Chosen

BY GOD

The
Little Brown One

WILLIE FRANCES HILL

KNOWLEDGE POWER BOOKS

ISBN: 978-09993455-9-7
Library of Congress Control Number: 2018942253

Edited by: Frank A. Williams
Literary Director: Sandra L. Slayton
Front and Back Cover Design: Juan Roberts, Creative Lunacy, Inc.

Published by:

Knowledge Power Books
A Division of Knowledge Power Communications, Inc.
Valencia, CA 91355
www.knowledgepowerbooks.com

Printed in the United States of America

Dedication

This book is dedicated to my beautiful daughter, Bridgitte, and my awesome sister, Florene. They both went home too soon.

Bridgitte was in the process of writing her book, so in some small way I hope that I put some of what she wanted to say in my book. I love you daughter, and I miss you so much. My sister, who I was cheated out of a chance to be with in our young adult life. I thank you for the love you showed us. We will meet again! R.I.P.

Florene and Husband

Bridgitte

Willie Frances

My Little Family

Left: My sister, Marie; Middle: my best friend, Earnestine, and my sister, Sweet Mae

Youngest sister, Pearl, holding her first born, Niecy. Better known as the hell raiser.

What happens when we're no longer able stand?

What really happens when we no longer have peace from our prayers?

What happens when we cannot accept the things we can?

What happens when wisdom is just not there to know the difference?

What happens when the hole is so big that purpose and meaning
is no longer a reason for living?

What happens when friends warm you with their presence and remember you in their
prayers and even then, you're unable to retain happiness?

By this time, you are closer to the bottom,
than where you should be moving to the top.

That's when we cry out to Jesus, help me, take me to the King
I don't have much to bring.

I am broken and only you can mend me back together again.

Renew my strength Lord,

Renew my spirit and create in me a clean heart.

Open my ears so I can hear when you call I will be forever in your presence.

Table of Contents

Love Notes
for
Willie (Fran)

ANDREA TISDALE

Great niece who broke the generational curse in our family. Loving and caring for her eight children.

"My aunt is a loving and caring, compassionate woman who has sacrificed time and time again for the sake of her family. She has never required acknowledgement for her deeds but deserves the world. She is the best "Mom/Aunt" I could have ever asked for."

TIA YANCEY

Youngest granddaughter who is the baby of the grands, who required much and later learned how to give back."

"My gram is like a mom to me growing up and coming to her house. She disciplined me the way I needed to be like a mom and taught me to do better. She was there and listened to me vent as much as I wanted. She also gave me advice whether I needed it or not. Taking her advice helped me a lot and when I didn't, it cost me."

EBONI

Middle granddaughter who was the make-up artist who used my first $50 bottle of Fashion Fair Foundation on her doll. That wasn't so good."

"My thoughts of my grandma as a child growing up. I looked at you as my connection to reality. You were one of the reasons we had any type of a chance at the happiness we had. It saved us from our heart's reality. It's crazy, because even as an adult, you're still that glue that connects us to everything, our foundation. You're the one who lets us know that it's more to life than what we were surrounded by and I'm thankful for you giving us a chance and I love you for that."

DONALD LEWIS YANCY

First grandchild who brought so much joy into our lives.

I am thinking of the memories we've made, and the love and faith we share, and the blessing of your example. I thank God every day that He made you my grandmother.

TONIE

Oldest granddaughter who had a mind of her own, then and now. I just had an epiphany. She is much like her mother, my daughter Bridgitte in many ways; strong and determined.

"Love this lady. My thoughts of you when we came to live with you. You always made sure we had lunch money every day. $2.00 to split four ways. Hard times, but happy times. Thanks for always being there for me as my grandma and as my friend."

SHAMIKA

Youngest niece who was a sweet innocent young girl who reminded me of myself as a child. I could see a reflection of me in her eyes. They were sad as mine at that age. I had to rescue her and bring some joy into her sad world.

"There's not enough words to express how if felt growing up with my Auntie Frances. I remember always wanting to be with her. She and I were traveling partners. We did everything together. If the car moved I was grabbing my coat. She changed my life to see the difference in people, but don't get me wrong. She didn't take no crap. She always made sure her family was taken care of. I looked up to her then and still to this day. I have a great role model and that is my Aunt Fran."

# Chapter One

FLORENE

The rain was dancing on the tin roof and tapping on the window pane in the room where I sat. I was thinking and reminiscing about the early stages of my childhood. I was thinking about how it all began and how I might make sense of it all. I thanked God for the rain because it soothed me as I eased on to the path I'd tried so hard to get away from. It was time, and I knew I had to go, I knew it was the only way I could put the pieces together. By doing this, I believed it would help me, not sure how other than being therapeutic. For the first time, I allowed myself to go back believing, "Faith is the substance of things hoped for; the evidence of things not seen." I am hopeful that my story will prove to be rewarding, and even cleansing for me from all the funky leftover baggage I've been carrying all these years.

I am a firm believer that we shouldn't let others tell our stories. The late Maya Angelou once said, "there is no greater agony than bearing an untold story inside you." I agree with her, so I shall tell of the excitement, sadness, laughter, and unforgettable moments.

I try hard to remember her face, but all I can see is the beautiful image of a happy angel. My eldest sister, Florene, that's what she was, a beautiful happy angel. When I think of her, I wished we had more time to have gotten to know each other. We were so young at the time, my older sister, Marie, and me. Though the time was far too little, I am grateful for the few summers we had together with her. We were always excited when it was time to be with her. Florene was so proud of us. I think she saw something good in us that came from the woman, our Mom who gave her up and walked out of her life. She very much wanted children of her own but was not able to carry full-term and would lose them a few months into her pregnancy. I saw her when she had lost a child and the hurt on her face stayed with me for many years.

During that time, we mourned for her child as they buried the baby in the yard being careful to put it deep enough to protect it from animals. I know now we were the best thing for her during those horrible times that robbed her of being a mother. God always says, "He never leaves or forsakes us and that He cares for us." God knew Florene needed to place some of the love she had for her stillborn child into Marie and I who needed the love. We were the joy she needed, and she was the light that pulled us out of the dark places we lived.

Florene lived in the country, near Jackson, Mississippi with her husband. She always enjoyed taking us to get our hair done. We would go to town, and she would buy new clothes for us. Her greatest joy was showing off her younger sisters and telling all the town's people we were visiting her for the summer. Those were our happiest times, the sheer joy and love that she showered us with, made us feel wanted for the first time in our little lives.

It was always sad when our time was over, and we had to go back to Memphis, Tennessee with Mom in that two-room back house. It was just a house to us; it was never home. The last time I saw my dear sister, she was on her way to California with her husband, who was in the military.

Florene and Mom didn't have a mother/daughter relationship. Mom left her with her father when she was five years old, and my sister never forgave her for it. Little did we know, we would be left as well. Mom and Florene were as different as day and night; even in features and skin tone. Florene was a few shades darker than me. My complexion is a light brown caramel, Florene was a dark brown mocha, and Mom was very light like her father, close to white. My great-grandfather was white and had many children by many different women from many different ethnicities. White, Black, and Cherokee Indian. My grandfather followed his father's footsteps. The story was that he was a rolling stone, "where ever he laid his hat was his home." A few wives and many different beautiful children. Mom kept him at a distance and wouldn't talk much about her past. I always felt that something happened when she was young, which is why she didn't have much love for him.

Mom was a beautiful lady. However, I don't believe she was ever meant to be a mother. She could be cold and callous at times and would leave Marie and me so many times with many different people before she started leaving us with Florene. I am grateful to God that we got to know Florene for a short time. It was like having an angel in some of the darkest times of our childhood. She was the only person in this world that we had to love us during that time other than my dear Aunt Ada. Mom had put distance between anyone that loved and wanted to take care of us. She took us away from Aunt Ada long before we started spending summers with Florene. Aunt Ada was my idol, and she loved us dearly. I remembered her being a praying woman of God. Aunt Ada was there when my Grandma who was sixteen died giving birth to Mom. It seemed Mom didn't want to abide by Aunt Ada's rules and teachings. Rather than doing the right thing, she would take off and we would end up staying with many different people. Some good, some not so good.

Suddenly Mom stopped taking us to our sister. She had a plan to get rid of us, not for a few summers, but for many years so she could be free. Because Mom's mother died during childbirth, she didn't have the motherly love or any reference to maternal instincts. You can't give what you don't have, and I don't ever remember her ever giving Marie or me a hug. Mom didn't want any of that or any of us.

The woman enjoyed her freedom too much to be tied down with babies and little young people who needed the care. Mom enjoyed partying and having men falling all over her, but the idea of being tied down and being a mother wasn't in the cards for her. She didn't know how to handle it and didn't want to learn. It took many years for me to forgive her for the hell she put us through. She had the spirit of carelessness, bitterness, resentment, and was very hateful. I am not sure she knew she had these issues or the characteristics that were causing her not to care. When situations got too sticky, she could always walk away, and she did so many times. The sad part was three of my sisters turned out just like her. I'll talk about that later. My sisters, too, had their babies and walked away from them. After many years of abuse and neglect. I finally had to admit to myself that Mom didn't know any better. Today I am at peace with that, though I must admit it did hurt and still does.

Now watch this chick's actions. (You will notice I refer to women as "chick" which is a slang I and many others used in my era. It's non-derogatory.) Mom walked away from her first child, Florene, leaving her with her father. She had a plan and was determined to win by any means necessary. She knew when she walked away, she would be footloose and fancy-free, and nothing would stop her. Mom had to persuade everyone that this was her only way out. She convinced people that she had no place to go and she couldn't take care of two small children. However, Mom could have left us with any number of capable family like, Florene or Aunt Ada. She even could have easily left us with family in Mississippi who, showed us love and care. But, she didn't want my sister or anyone to know she was walking away and giving us up, so she decided to take the less complicated way out for her, and more complicated for us.

Chapter Two

WILLIE WALLS: "THE GIANT"

Mom began to execute her plan. We were all at Mrs. Elizabeth's house, she was a good friend of Willie Walls who was one of Mom's occasional boyfriends. Gladys, Mrs. Elizabeth's friend, was there, too. Mom was telling Willie Walls and his friends that he was our dad. He, on the other hand was saying, "Mamma's baby, daddy's maybe." Although Marie and I were there, they were holding a meeting and talking about us as if we weren't in the room. The heated conversation was to persuade Willie Walls to let us stay with him. He was fighting for his freedom and saying he was not our father.

They continued persuading Willie Walls for a very long time and finally weighing him down. His argument was Marie wasn't his because the timing was off. As for me, I could've been. From what I gathered, Mom was in and out of the relationship, but never staying too long, and then move on making it doubtful that we were his children.

In the end, the women won, and Willie Walls agreed to care for us for a short time, which ended up being more than five years. I think Mom could have won him over by herself but having the other two women on her side guaranteed the win. Willie Wall's best friends helped her sealed the deal. The three women sticking together was no match for him, he didn't have a chance. She was a restless spirit, and it was hard for her to stay grounded for long. Mom just couldn't stand the responsibility of raising children.

I can only remember seeing her once or twice, during the five-plus years. Like most children, regardless of how awful their Mom may be, they love their Mom. I thought she was so pretty and I loved her even though she left us with "the Giant."

I just wanted a mother and craved it. I always prayed she would come back for us, but she never did.

Willie Walls was a giant of a man, very dark features, bald, and looked angry all the time. I guess I would be angry, too, if I was suckered into taking care of two small children. I still don't remember seeing him smile when I was a child or even now. Getting settled in with this man, we knew nothing about was very scary for both of us. He showed us where we would be sleeping, and then we were all alone in a house with an unfriendly giant. He didn't want us there and didn't care if we knew it. He told us we would be enrolling in school. I'm not sure who took us to enroll in school. I do know our clothes weren't the best and we felt out of place altogether. Down the street from our school was the high school, George Washington High School, where Florene told us she graduated. That was the only time I remember a little joy, knowing my sister had gone there and being close to her past. On our way home from school, we would run up the many steps and sit there wishing we were with Florene again. We were hoping we could see her face and hearing her tell all her friends how much she loved her sisters. When you are so unhappy, you'll grab whatever piece of happiness you could get.

Meanwhile, we were trying to fit in, and learning survival skills at our young age. We were teaching ourselves to cook and fend for ourselves. I believe God had our angels watching over us because there was no way we could have made it on our own. However, it wasn't too long before I started to rebel. I didn't like anything this man was dishing out. Once we were in school, he told us we had to start going to church.

We were introduced to our second home, New Hope Baptist Church, a small wood frame church, painted white on the outside, but colorful on the inside. The congregation was very small, probably no more than 100 members, if that many. He kept us at church as much as he could to get us out of the house. We were made to go to church every Wednesday, Sunday, and other time they had something going on. We would go out the front door, and he would have his women coming in the back door. He couldn't wait to get rid of us so that he could do his thing. It was ok with us because the church was a place of refuge. It was a joy to go to church. We begun to meet other kids in the neighborhood. The Mothers, who wore their white dresses and hats, felt sorry for us and showed us love and affection. They knew we were little-lost souls without the proper parental covering. The church was our peace and sanctuary. My favorite scripture is (Jeremiah 29:11 NIV). "For I know the plans I have for you, declares the LORD, plans to prosper you and not to harm you, plans to give you a hope and a future."

God is so awesome that our first church would have hope in its name and for us, it was our new hope. It was our hope for our sad little existence. New Hope was a home that embraced us and gave us the peace and hope that was mentioned in Jeremiah 29:11. Somehow, it felt like the curse on our lives was being broken. We were ministered to by our Pastor and the Mothers of the church. They even prepared us for baptism. They were our parents making sure we understood and knew the Lord, and what confessing Jesus as our Lord and Savior meant as best they could. I am taking a moment to thank God for New Hope Baptist Church and all who brought light to us as we knew nothing but darkness and sadness. My God and Father knew we would gain strength, wisdom, be loved, comforted, and learn more about God while we were there.

Time passed, and my rebellion kicked in strong. I started getting into trouble by not coming in the house on time. If we went someplace like to the movie theatre, I would always stay away too long. When we would get in trouble, "the Giant" would whip my sister much harder than me. Though he knew I was the one that didn't want to come home, he always beat her and gave me a few taps. This treatment went on for some time. I can remember at least four times that he whipped her and tapped me.

Chapter Three

CHOSEN BY GOD

Easter was coming, and our church was putting on a play, "Footsteps of Jesus." The Children's Ministry team drew and cut out footprints for us to walk in. Walking in Jesus' steps was the best. The feeling was transforming, and for the first time, I felt safe. We didn't have money for clothes, and "the Giant" didn't seem to care. Marie and I were playing near a bus stop, and we saw a small purse on the bench that someone had left. An angel maybe, so we opened it, and money was inside. We were so happy and went to our stepmom, Ms. Jesse, and asked if she could help us with an Easter outfit. She said it wasn't enough to buy dresses, but she could get material and make our dresses, and she did. I will never forget how happy we were to get new dresses. It had been a long time since we had anything new. God always knows how to bring light in a dark place. Walking in Jesus' footprints, finding the purse, and new dresses were our Easter miracle.

On that glorious day, I was so happy and at the same time sad, that I didn't have a father. You would think that I would think of Mom, but she had been absent from our lives so much that I was used to not having her around. Looking at the children with their fathers made my heart ache. I had this feeling once before when Mom left us, and now I was feeling it again. It was a physical pain that hurt to the core, and there was nothing I could do to soothe it. Then God spoke to my spirit and said, "From this day on, you will never have to be without a father. I am your Father, and if you acknowledge me, I will direct your path."

It was my first encounter with God. I was chosen by our Lord and Savior to be His child. As a young child, I didn't quite understand what was happening, but from that moment, I was a different person. I was totally transformed, and I wasn't sad anymore. There was a newness in me at the tender young age of eleven, and I knew I had been chosen by God to be His child, so it no longer mattered to me about that piece of man wasn't a daddy, father or anything personal to me. I knew I had a Father and I felt I was removed from the horrible and lonely life we were in, even if nothing had changed, it didn't bother me anymore.

I no longer had the mind of an eleven-year-old child. However, I continued to be rebellious, and my sister would feel the effects. I never knew or understood the reason why "the Giant" hated Marie much more than he hated me. I didn't know what was going on, but one night he took Marie out of the house. It was the night I lost my sister. It was the night, "the Giant" allowed his best friend to rape Marie. She was thirteen years old. Marie was frightened and never got over that painful night. I hated him for what he allowed to happen to her and I knew one day I would have to get me and my sister away from that madness. She was a couple of years older than me, but I played the big sister's role. I thought we were safe, but after that night, we both were scared for our lives.

Sometime later, I can't remember what we did but "the Giant" beat Marie again. He tapped me a few times and beat the crap out of her. He broke her wrist, and this time and I couldn't hold my tongue. I was going to tell "the Giant" just what I was holding inside of me even if it killed me. I stood on the edge of the bed, looked him in his eyes, and called him every name I could bring up out of my mouth. I told him just what I thought of him for allowing his friend to rape Marie and the beatings he would give her. It was the first time Ms. Jesse heard this, she was confused, crying, and not knowing what the hell was going on.

I told him if he ever touched her again that I would kill him in his sleep. Ms. Jesse was crying saying, "Willie Frances, he is going to hurt you." I told her, "you couldn't pay this ugly, piece of man to touch me." It was something in my eyes that told him to back off, and I wasn't afraid. I was very calm; my eyes said it all. At twelve, I had power, and he knew it. He saw something, and he didn't want to mess with me. I told him if he didn't take her to the hospital I would call the police and report him. Ms. Jesse kept crying along with Marie. He finally got his act together and took her to the hospital.

Ms. Jesse was a good-hearted woman and tried to help as much as possible. She came into the picture a few years after we were there and didn't see much of the damage. She lived partially in "the Giant's" house and at her home, so she wasn't there all the time. It was great on the days when Ms. Jesse was there because it was always happy times. Of all "the Giants" different women, Ms. Jesse was the one that was good in heart and spirit and tried to show she cared.

After that crazy flare-up with the beating of Marie, I started to plot our getaway. I knew we had to go. I was never afraid after my encounter with God because He said He would direct my path. Shortly after the wrist deal, I still felt the strength that I could do what I needed to do, and I would have God with me. I knew the power of prayer, and I knew how to pray. It was all I had, and it was enough. I woke up a few months later and told my sister it was time to go. She asked, "go where?" I told her we would hitchhike to the other side of town and try to find Mom. She started to freak out, jumping up and down saying he would hurt her. Just seeing that raw fear that he had put in her made me angry.

That rebellious spirit rose up in me, and I went into action. I began vandalizing the house. I was breaking things, running water everywhere, breaking eggs on the walls, and putting ashes in his bed, on his beautiful white sheets. That built-up anger was coming out. Marie was bawling hard then; I told her to shut up, and to pack the few clothes we had. After feeling like I had made him feel as bad as he made us feel, we headed out. I didn't have a clue which way to go or what direction to go in. There was no plan. I just knew we had to get away. Finally, we were making a mad dash to get as far away from that house as we could. We were headed to our Mom's house because we had heard "the Giant" describe where Mom was living. I knew we would not return to his house.

By the grace of God, we managed to get several rides, mostly with white women. Some curious, some nosy, and some angels that were sent to help us. I am sure they felt sorry for us, seeing two young girls hitch-hiking. I was twelve and Marie was fourteen. As I write this, I am seeing the love and respect Marie had for me all those years. It never dawned on me how she felt about me. I knew she loved me as my other two sisters came to love and respect me. With Marie, I had to be there for her. I fought her battles with the crazy bad kids. I was always there for her. Then after years with "the Giant," I had to rise up against him and free my sister from the torture she endured. Looking back, I never had a regular kid's life. My mind was always in survival mode.

We made it to the house on Carpenter Street. The house belonged to my Aunt Mattie, and Mom had the two rooms in the back of her house. By the time we reached Mom, we were surprised to see she had two more kids. Both girls, had a look of shock on their faces, and Mom was asking where and how? I looked her in the eyes and said, "we hitchhiked." I asked if she could take care of us, and if she couldn't, we would continue to Detroit where Aunt Ada lived. Aunt Ada was the one that used to try to encourage Mom about taking care of us when we were very young. She was living in Mississippi at the time, and later moved to Detroit, so her son could care for her.

Mom robbed us of Aunt Ada's love by not going to see her because she didn't want to hear Ada Steward telling her to take better care of us. I loved my Aunt; she was a God-fearing woman. I have reason to believe that Ada's prayers for me have been in many ways, very potent. I believed they covered me when death was at my door. The effectual fervent prayers of the righteous avails much. I know that God has, in many ways, taken me under His care, guidance, provision, and protection. I believe He is honoring her prayers for my family and me, as well as keeping His word in directing my path.

Later we told Mom what had happened and the damage that I had done to the "the Giant's" house, and that we could never go back. It didn't take Mom but a minute to say yes to us, she was happy as hell. Mom was elated because she had two teenagers to wash nasty, funky diapers, and clean and care for her young babies. She didn't take care of us but demanded us to care for her children, and if we didn't do something right, she would beat us. Mom was vicious and crazy as hell and didn't care one bit. She introduced us to a new meaning of hell. Mom showed her true colors, her real face. She didn't say no to us staying because she knew she had someone to take care of her children and clean. I didn't mind; I was always praying that if I help her, she would maybe like me a little bit and come to love me one day. Right!

Marie and I were trying to adjust with five people living in a two-room back house, with a bathroom across the hall. Cramped, but we tried to be happy. Mom did not want us, and sometimes she didn't mind telling us. One night I woke up and went looking for her. She was outside at the gate, and I asked, "Mom, what are you doing out here?" She turned and looked me in the face and told me she wished she never had me. She said, "she wished she didn't have any of us. There was that pain again, the physical pain that cuts to the core. You would think I would have been used to rejection. I would ask myself, *"What is wrong with me? How could you say those things to me? I am the only one who loves you."* Thank God that He is close to the brokenhearted and saves those crushed in spirit (Psalm 34:18 NIV) and (Psalm 27:10 NIV). When my father and mother forsake me, the Lord will take me up. I believed this.

Time passed as we got used to taking care of our new responsibilities. Marie was not that much help. By this time, she just didn't care. Mentally, she had checked out from the bad experience she had with "the Giant" and his friend. Looking back, I saw her in need of someone to talk to, someone to scream with, and allow her to cry. Marie was hurting inside and couldn't tell anyone. There was no one around to help her. She wanted someone to know, that she had been violated and raped at the age of thirteen, and there was no one to hold her but me. We had to be there for each other in those frightful times. We were young girls in a world that wasn't good to us. I am crying as I write this, surely you understand why I never want to visit this part of my life.

When we were in school, Marie had kids trying to beat her up from time to time. There were many fights. She was very light in complexion, and the darker girls were after her. Back in our time, there was a black and high yellow thing going on. I didn't mind fighting. I was always mad at the cruel situation we were in, so fighting worked for me. When the bunch would be picking fights with Marie, I would always be trying to get to her and help her. When they would see me coming, they would take off, and if they were still there when I got to her, I would try to beat them down. I had a way of winning. I fought hard and I was never afraid, whether it was one or five, the fight was on.

One day it was too many, and I jumped in, got them off Marie and we had to take off running. They followed me all the way to the back of the house. As we made it inside, they were yelling for me to come out. We had a chamber pot, to hold our urine or defecation, that we used at night and dumped in the morning before going to school. That morning we didn't dump it out. As they were yelling, "Willie Frances come out!" I told Marie to open the door and when she did I, splashed the overnight pee all over their butts. They parted like the Red Sea, stinking like funk in their hair and clothing. From that moment on, they never messed with Marie or me again.

There were so many sad and unhealthy times but knowing there is no greater agony than bearing an untold story, I know I made the right decision to write my life story. I thought it was my idea to tell it until I got to the part where I was ashamed, and I didn't want to share it. God revealed to me that it wasn't even about me but about the promise that He made to me, to never leave or forsake me. He said that the testimony was to be a blessing to others.

Meanwhile, I believed and still believe no child should have to go through suffering and neglect. However, it is the hand that some are dealt. The condition of your birth does not determine the outcome of your life. There we were, with Mom, who I started calling, "the crazy woman," who had dumped us for many years and now we were back, and she was not happy. It didn't take her long to get over the excitement of having us there, to care for her and her children. Marie wasn't bothered by her at all, because she had turned the world off. Marie took a vacation from life and the woman we called Mom. Putting it in the proper perspective, Marie just didn't give a damn. Mom had beaten us bad earlier because somebody had eaten a couple of pieces of her chocolate covered cherries. Marie finally admitted eating the candies, and she beat her until she was sick and vomiting, even though she had put a mean one on me. My heart hurt at the idea of getting beaten so vicious over some candy; it just didn't make sense. But nothing did. Even to this day, I hate to look at a chocolate covered cherry.

Marie had already tuned out on life, and that beating took her completely out. She never changed, even when she got married and had children. Marie was happy on the outside, but I don't think she ever got to be the person she was before all the abuse and ugliness. She was robbed of the woman God called her to be, and Marie ended up being like the woman who birthed her. She had two beautiful girls, Eunice and Fran and was never the mother to them she should've been. All of us could have been better mothers. Some of us are just gifted to take on more substantial roles. As her daughters grew up, they started portraying the same behavior as Marie, not caring about many things. Generational curses are what I call it.

After Marie checked out, I had to handle most of the housework duties as well as taking care of my younger sisters, Mae, the oldest and Pearl, the youngest. They were not nice, sweet little girls, they were just the opposite. They cried all the time, threw their bottles at you, and had funky attitudes. They took after their mama, my mama. When Mae and Pearl grew older, things only got worse. Mom made a difference in how she treated us. I felt the brunt of the difference because I was a few shades darker than they were. I was different, and they let me know it. I was labeled black girl or black thing. I had been called black so much that I really thought I was dark when I was a little brown girl. Mae and Pearl heard Mom calling me those names, so they would do it, too. When they were older and ready for a rude awakening and a royal butt whipping, I put a stop to the black thing and anything else that I didn't like about them. They were still bad, but they had much more respect for me. I turned that black thing into black love. In the end, they loved and respected me as a mother figure.

Chapter Four

OUR NEW FAMILY

Mom was restless and started telling us about her father. It was the first time we had heard anything about her father. The next thing we knew, we were going to meet him and the Collins Family. Mom contacted him, and he sent bus tickets for all of us to come and meet our family in Mississippi. Now we were not sure how to take all of this as Mom was always full of surprises. One thing was for sure, we were on our way to Winona, Mississippi.

Winona, Mississippi, is in Montgomery county, located 86 miles north of Jackson, Mississippi (center to center) and is 116 miles south of Memphis, Tennessee. The city of Winona derived its name from a Sioux word which meant "first-born daughter."

Mom hadn't told us that her father was mixed, so when the bus pulled into the station, I said, "Granddaddy is not here to pick us up." Mom pointed to a big fellow looking like Paul Drake, the private investigator on the T.V. show, *Perry Mason*. I said, "Mom, he's a white man." She said, "that is your granddaddy." When he saw us, he came over, and introduced himself to us. He looked a bit confused, and we must have looked like some poor kids looking pitiful in our best clothes. We got in the car, and we were on our way. Granddaddy told my aunt to get in touch with Shawn Trice right away. She was a well-known, excellent seamstress in Winona, Mississippi.

The next day all of us were measured for a week's worth of clothes. It turned out, Ms. Trice had made each of us a beautiful sunback dress for the party that was taking place later that night. I thought it was all a dream, and I would wake up in the same old clothes. Granddaddy was having a big celebration for his daughter and grandchildren who had come home. Relatives came from all directions. The huge yard, packed with cars, trucks, wagons, and long tables were filled with many platters of delicious food. I nearly fainted when I saw the spread. I had never seen so much food, and it was probably obvious, because we ate our little selves to no end. It was a night to remember, meeting Mom's brothers and sisters and their children.

I kept asking myself, *"Why didn't Mom tell us about our family?"* I couldn't understand how all these people, our new family was showing us so much love, and they weren't poor like us. Granddaddy had money and everybody bearing that name had money. My Grandfather's father was white and very rich. Rumor had it, he owned a significant portion of Winona, and he took care of all his children; the whites, blacks, and Indians. It was a rainbow family. They were beautiful people and wanted us to be a part of them. I found out there were more relatives, but we were only there for a week and didn't get a chance to meet all of them. My favorite uncle was Lynn, and he had two sons named Lynn, Jr. and Tom. Ruby, one of Uncle Lynn's daughters, was very sweet and seemed to work harder than the rest. She helped Aunt Mary run the house and cooked all that good food. I just knew I was dreaming and never wanted it to end.

Lynn, Jr. and Tom took us horseback riding every day and showed us the beautiful, green country-side. I had only seen these things on a black and white TV with all the actors and actresses being white. But there we were, riding on a beautiful, trained mare that looked like a show horse, with a white star on his head. Thinking back, that's when I discovered my love for horses. It was the one time that my sister, Marie, was happy. She loved riding Tom's big mare. Both of us were scared to mount them, but the guys were so gentle with us, we trotted until we got the hang of holding tight, then they took off like we were at the race track. They loved racing each other. It was sheer exhilaration and breathtaking. I will never forget those happy times.

While the guys did all the chores, one of my cousins, Paulette, showed us the girly things around the farm. Sometimes, Uncle Lynn would start conversations with me, and I would ask questions. He explained things to me, and I liked sitting at his feet when he shared with me. He asked me questions about our living conditions in Memphis. I guess, Uncle Lynn, probably knew we weren't living under the best conditions in Memphis. Maybe he had heard rumors, I'm not sure how he knew and maybe he felt safer asking me than Mom. It appeared that they loved Mom and the family were closer to Mom than we knew.

Suddenly, it was time to go home. The dream was coming to an end. Wake up, wake up! The last night before we left, we went to a drive-in movie theater. Some packed in the cab, and some were in the back of the big truck, having loads of fun. Then Lynn said, the Ku Klux Klan (KKK) was on the road up ahead. I could see the white robes and hoods. I had never seen anything like that before. I thought maybe Memphis wasn't so bad after all. Lynn said, "hold on..." It was clear that he had no intentions of stopping for the white-hooded Klansmen. One of them shouted, "that's the Collins's boys, let them through." Those hooded men let us through, no trouble. The Collins name still carried a lot of power. The Klan would burn crosses at the bottom of the hill of Uncle Lynn's home, but he said, "you couldn't pay them crackers to come up that hill." The Klansmen wanted to scare the Collins, but they knew not to hurt them.

Later I asked my cousin, was he scared. He said, "I got a shotgun under the seat, and two forty-fives in the glove compartment." They were some bad boys for sure who weren't scared at all. I guess they had encountered them before. Uncle Lynn shared with me that the KKK threatened him for marching with Dr. Martin Luther King, Jr., but he was packing ammunition and wasn't scared to use it. My great grandfather's name carried all of them. Again, they could threaten them, but they couldn't harm them or kill them.

Granddaddy and Uncle Lynn had spent hours trying to convince Mom to stay in Winona. They promised Mom she would never have to worry about anything again. They would build her a home and provide all that Mom needed plus help get us into school. In the end, she said no, and we rode off with precious memories, leaving family, food, beauty, and most of all family love. Mom didn't tell us why, and we knew not to keep asking, she could slap real fast, and you never could figure out what you did or said, so you just knew to shut up, and keep it moving.

Although we couldn't ask any questions, I was wondering what would make a woman walk away from a much better life, plus a family that loved her and wanted to help her family? What would make her say no?

I missed Uncle Lynn most. He was a very delightful, warm, and an intelligent man. I thought the world of him, and it was apparent to everyone that he enjoyed talking with me, too. I got in touch with him by phone many years later and I told him I was one of Florence's daughter. I asked him if he knew who I was? He said, "You're that little brown one." I was so touched that he remembered me and recognized my voice after nearly fifty years. I told him I was coming to see him, but unfortunately 9/11 attacks happened. (9/11 was a series of four coordinated terrorist attacks by the Islamic terrorist group al-Qaeda on the United States on the morning of Tuesday, September 11, 2001. The attacks killed 2,996 people, injured more than 6,000 others, and caused at least $10 billion in infrastructure and property damage.)

Uncle Lynn's health was failing, but still able to get around, and I begged him to please stay healthy long enough for us to physically connect one more time. He promised. That promise was kept as he and I were able to reconnect and I had a wonderful time with him. He passed a couple of months after our visit.

During this visit, I found out Mom had made trips down there before and after she had left us with "the Giant." When I discovered her secret,

I was so hurt, I cried all the way back home, big buckets of tears. I said to myself, *"Yes Mom, I have busted your butt. Why couldn't you have taken us to be with our family rather than giving us to 'the Giant' and not caring how we were cared for and treated. You trusted this man to take care of your precious young girls. Well, I guess your freedom was more important than doing the right thing."*

I was so thankful that I had the opportunity to see Uncle Lynn and that he took the time to spend with me. I was grateful to him for providing sweet lasting memories. I believe we both made a unique impression on one another. I thank God for those days. Uncle Lynn was the first man whom I admired and was proud to know. Our visit with our family gave us a chance to dream and feel the warmth and love of a family that Marie and I never had. God knew I would need the knowledge of knowing who we were, where we came from, who guided us, and gave us hope. Rest in peace, dear uncle.

Chapter Five

BACK IN MEMPHIS

We returned home and to the beans and gravy. Not long after we made it back to Memphis, Mom found us a three-room shotgun house. A shotgun house is a narrow, rectangular residence, with rooms arranged one behind the other and doors at each end of the house. Basically, you go from the living room, take a few steps, and you're in the bedroom, another step, and you're in the kitchen and bathroom. It was our best yet. Marie and I shared the living room and Mom and the girls shared the bedroom. We were living large. Honestly, it was truly a blessing. We were dirt poor and didn't have much food and shopped at second-hand stores for our clothes. We were happy for a little while. I was always praying and hoping we could make Mom happy, so she would love and want us.

One day, Mom woke up and found she was out of coffee. Being an avid coffee drinker and without it was not good. I wanted Mom to have her coffee. So, I started thinking of a way to get her some coffee. Later that day, while skipping through the alley, I found a five-dollar bill. I rushed to the store and brought Mom some coffee and couldn't wait to give it to her to make her happy. I thought maybe she would hug me. Right! She took the coffee, and to this day, I can't remember Mom ever saying thank you. It was alright, though, because God sent an angel to make sure I was happy. The fact that I was able to give her the coffee brought joy to me.

There was always a shortage of food at home. It took a great amount of strength to drum up excitement when I would come home for dinner. I grew weary of the same menu: beans, cornbread, and gravy. My face smiled, "Yum," but my heart said, "not again." I decided to do some babysitting for a wealthy white family. Not long after I started, the woman asked if I wanted to do house cleaning. I quickly said yes, thinking more money; I was ready. Their home was in a very prominent neighborhood, one of the wealthiest in Memphis. The lawns were professionally manicured, and their beautiful cars were parked in their driveway. I had never seen anything in Memphis I could identify with, such as what real money could buy. It was an eye-opener to allow myself to dream.

The woman began to give me a list of the many things she wanted me to do. I thought to myself, *it is only one of me and I just weighted about 98lbs.* Then she said, "When you clean the floors, do it on your hands and knees with a pad, brush, and bucket. Then put the wax on the same way." My mind was racing, not understanding why on earth would she want this little cute, underweight, 14-year-old brown girl to do all that she was asking. I just couldn't understand it. She had already told me that I was intelligent and spoke like I lived up North. Everything was yes and no, rather than yes ma'am and no ma'am. As I think about it now, she probably didn't appreciate my speaking to her like I had some sense and held my head up high like I was somebody. With clear feelings, I was sure that I would never clean a white woman's house in the South or anywhere. I just kept thinking, *there's got to be a better way.*

My heart just wasn't in it. On top of it, she was throwing out all those outrageous demands, and she seemed to be feeling like she was going to work the heck out of me. But I had something in mind, too. As soon as she left the house, I grabbed the mop and went over her already clean floors and hit and missed everything. I didn't give a dang about her and her house. I knew if I could help it, I would not be coming back this way ever again. I had an ache in my heart that another human being wouldn't care about a child, a mature child trying to earn a little money. I was beginning to see the outside world like the one I lived in, cold and heartless. Some folks don't know how to care. Lord, have mercy on them.

I was always thinking of ways to bring some money in the house. My next venture was in Arkansas to chop and pick cotton. I can talk about both, being that I chopped and picked, and hated them both. Marie and I would have to get up real early in the mornings and wait for a bus that picked us up along with other cotton pickers and choppers. The bus took us from Memphis across the Arkansas Bridge to West Memphis, to the area in the country where all could be seen were rows of cotton. Chopping cotton was brutal because of the long rows in the hot sun all day long. I wasn't good at either one, and I didn't get much done. Picking cotton wasn't any fun, either, both were terrible. My fingers had pricks on them, and I was bent over all day long. Good Lord! The people who had to do this for a living, or was made to do it, had to be miserable. The big tall, black guys could pick 500 lbs. of cotton in a day which is a lot because cotton is light. I was fascinated with them by the way they did their job. The most I could pick was 35 to 40 lbs. and sometimes there was mud with the cotton. I would get sick of looking at it and not seeing any money. I would get balls of mud and pack cotton around it. Marie would put on red lipstick, and the brothers, loving high yellow women, would be in line to pick her a 100 lbs. after they finished picking theirs. I was over it.

I knew there was a better way, so I started stealing. I would walk in the front door of the market and fill a bag with groceries and walk out the side door. I wouldn't give it a second thought. I wasn't afraid, I was just hungry. It was a natural thing for me to do. I would tell Mom the money I was making was from babysitting. She didn't ask many questions, and I didn't volunteer any information.

Stealing became a way of life for me for a minute. Then I met my first real friend, Susie, and she was a thief for real. Susie stole everything. She showed me how to go in the department stores and steal clothes. I became a pro real fast. Eventually, my friend got caught stealing and the whole school found out about it. It was the talk around town. She didn't have to steal; her Mom was a beautician and they lived well. She stole because deep inside she enjoyed it and she did it to help me. Meanwhile, I was still thinking to myself that there had to be a better way. After she got caught, I slowed down and found another way to get money.

There were nasty old men in the neighborhood that owned small businesses. One of them was a fruit and vegetable vendor who did his business from his wagon. There was another one who owned a fish market. These old men were always talking to young girls very disrespectful. I figured out a way to get them all. I would set Marie up with them, pretending to be interested. While she entertained them, I would sneak in and steal their money. The owner of the fish market was such a tramp, he had a mattress in the backroom and was always trying to get young girls, women, or anybody he could to go in the backroom. I would have Marie take him to the backroom to play and pretend like she was going to give it up and I would steal his premium fish. Mom was always sending us up there for the funky fish heads and she would make fish head stew and sometimes bake them. It was a break from the gravy and bread and we ate well a few days with the prime fish.

The dirty old men knew I was stealing from them and threatened to tell Mom. But I didn't care if they told on me. If so, I would expose their old horny ways. All the old men in the neighborhood got robbed by me. I had Marie entertain them in the living room while I climbed through the window and stole their money and whatever valuables I could use. I didn't feel anything, and they couldn't tell anyone because I would let the world know just how nasty they were. I felt like they got what they deserved.

Chapter Six

MOM'S MASTER PLAN

Marie was dating a guy in the neighborhood named Dee, and she was in love with him. She was happy for a while until she met Eddie. He was older, very popular, and a singer. When he sang at our school's talent shows, the girls would go wild. He liked Marie, and everybody was shocked that he would pick a nobody since he had a chance to be with rich girls. Eddie was coming to the house and Mom loved him more than Dee.

Mom put a plan in motion to get Marie married. Dee got pushed to the back of the bus and, eventually, out of the picture. Marie loved dating a guy that everybody else wanted, and Eddie chose her, but deep inside she loved Dee and didn't know how to say, "Stop this merry go round and let me off." I loved Eddie as well because I got attention by him dating my sister.

Mom was setting Marie up for marriage and I had no idea. When Marie got pregnant, Mom rushed the wedding. However, Marie was still tipping with Dee from time to time, and I believed Dee was the father. Later in their marriage, Eddie realized it, and many problems led to their divorce after their second child was born. It wasn't a marriage made in heaven. It was all for the wrong reason.

I started hanging out with a set of twins, Pauline and Irene, who were a year older than me. The twins were in a much better financial shape than me, but their family didn't have a lot, either. Plus, they were more mature in life than I was. The one thing we had in common was they loved to fight like I did. I got into many fights because some of the little, well-to-do girls didn't want to have anything to do with us. We were poor, and we knew it. It was fine if they didn't treat me as if I was beneath them, and when they did, the fight was on. We got into a lot of trouble fighting. They set me up to start the scuffle and the twins would step in and finish it.

Things heated up when the Yancey boys, Joe, Roy, and Napoleon, moved in town from the country. These brothers were handsome, and they had their act together, so we thought. The twins started to date the older ones, and sometimes I would sneak out and hang ten with Joe, the youngest. Joe was nine years older than me, which made life somewhat challenging. Pauline was dating Roy and Irene was dating Napoleon. What Irene didn't know was Napoleon was also dating Barbara. Napoleon was having fun for a few months, but Barbara got pregnant and Barbara's mother was upset. She had some words with Napoleon and arranged their wedding. Irene shed many tears because was in love with Napoleon.

I was dating Joe, and he was good to Mom and me. Joe put money in my pocket and food on the table. Mom didn't mind Joe being much older than me. She focused on what he could bring to the table. Mom had already married Marie off and had a plan in mind to rid herself of me yet again. When I prostituted myself and brought money home from this older man, she was happy. I thought she and I had gotten over the rough edges and she was pleased having me around. It was okay when I was stealing and feeding them, and keeping a quart of beer for her, she was happy. However, I was wrong again. She was setting me up for a letdown.

I got pregnant and thought I was hiding it up to my fifth month. Just around that time, I walked in the house, and heard Mom and Joe speaking of someone getting married. I asked, "who's getting married?" Mom responded, "you are! I know you're pregnant and Joe has agreed to marry you." I felt betrayed, trapped, and cornered. Probably what a guy feels when he gets a girl pregnant but doesn't want to get married. I screamed, "I don't want to get married, I want to have the baby and finish school!" Mom said, "Joe has agreed to let you go back and finish." I asked her, "Why can't I stay with you?" She wasn't having any of that and little did I know at the time, that chick was planning her get-away again and heading to Detroit. That restless spirit wasn't staying down any longer as our marriages had afforded her an opportunity to make her get-away. I agreed to the wedding. I didn't believe I had a choice whatsoever.

One of the twins had gotten married, and the other one was engaged, so they were helping me with my shotgun wedding. (A shotgun wedding is a wedding that is arranged or forced into marriage due to an unplanned pregnancy.) I ordered myself a red wedding dress from a catalog. All the weddings I had experienced, were house weddings and the men would go in the kitchen after the ceremony, drink up all the liquor and I wasn't feeling like I wanted this to be a part of my wedding. I ran away from "the Giant" at twelve, and now at fifteen, a wedding was in the mix. I was angry, hurt, and I felt like I had traveled this road before. Rage was building inside me and my defense mechanism started to kick in. It was danger! Danger! The anger could have been hazardous to my life. When I felt this way in the past, it resulted in me heading into something that I have no control over. I knew nothing about taking care of a grown man who was nine years older than me. I made a mistake, and this is how I must pay for it. It was indeed a season in my life that I had no clue of the outcome. I was in the 9th grade, pregnant, and my mama was marrying me off. She had no concern of what the result would be for me. My friends were taking care of everything for the wedding for me because I was lifeless. I understood how my sister felt when she checked out and was just going through the motions.

A few friends and I were sitting out front of the shotgun houses. The girl next door had a little too much wine to drink, and she started cussing.

Marie had just come home from the hospital after having her first child which was a girl. I was holding the baby, and the chick cursed again. I said, "Don't talk that way...my Mom can hear you." She did it again. I said to her, "Please don't do this." She said, "F??? you and your Mom." Those were fighting words. I loved my Mom and sisters, even if they didn't care for me like that. I was still going to love them regardless. I placed the baby in somebody's lap and knocked that chick out of her chair. When she realized what happened, she was ready for a fight. We rolled in the dirt and dust for the longest time. Finally, someone shouted that the police were coming. I ran into my house and she was still screaming the same crap. I was headed out the back door when a quart size beer bottle missed my head. I picked up the bottle and laid one on her, splitting her head open and blood went everywhere. She charged at me like a wild bull. It scared me. I was determined to quickly to put an end to the madness. I got her in a headlock and told her I would choke the life out of her if she didn't settle down.

I could hear the police sirens and Marie yelling; "My sister is bleeding and hurt." Marie thought I was bleeding because my clothes were full of blood, but I wasn't the one bleeding. I was trying to tell Marie what was going on. I released that chick and ran back in the house to clean myself up. Within minutes, I was completely transformed from the wet, bloody, dusty, ragged girl to this beautiful brown girl in the pretty red dress I had ordered for my wedding. The police were at the door screaming, "Willie Frances, come out." I opened the door and stepped out. I always could make something good of a bad situation. You could hear and see the crowd in total disbelief. I could've received an Oscar for this role. I was in character and doing my very first red-carpet walk.

The police questioned if I was involved in the fight. I answered that I was. The officers looked at me in my pretty red dress, hair combed, with a look of disbelief. The chick I was fighting look like she had been whipped with an ugly stick. In the end, they took us both to the juvenile authorities. We were both fifteen and pregnant. The chick was still carrying on with her threats which held no weight, but it was when I saw racism at its worse. The white cop turned to look at us in the back seat and said to me, "the next time this nigger bitch bothers you, kill the black bitch." I was in shock and hurt very badly. For a cop to say these awful words, I couldn't believe it. I was sad and wanted to cry for her. To be spoken to like that at such a young age by nasty, racist cops who didn't give a damn about black people; was a hard slap in my face. I don't believe these cops had witnessed a case like this before. They had never met a pretty, young brown girl who, minutes earlier, had been in an ugly, bloody fight, and then in their presence speaking and looking damn good.

We stayed in the juvenile facility for a week. It was the third time I was involved in fights. If this had happened in school, most times, my principal would speak on my behalf and as a result, with good behavior, the discipline was light. My principal understood me and saw something good in me. This time he couldn't help me. They charged me with assault and battery. The judge told me if I came back in his court again he would send me to the big house. The chick and I made up as soon as we got in our cells. I had forgiven her and was sensitive to her because the police spoke to her like she was nothing. I wasn't mad anymore, and we were okay when we got out. We didn't see much of each other after that. I married and moved to the projects. Yes, that was moving up. It was big time compared to the shotgun house. Plus, they were practically new.

The day of the wedding, I wore somebody's blue prom dress, my friends had gotten me because the pretty red dress I ordered from the catalog, I put it on after the fight and wore it when I was taken to juvenile hall. Our neighborhood beautician, Ms. Alice agreed to do my hair. Everybody was so good to me and when it was all said and done, I was made into a beautiful princess. The transformation was mind-blowing for me, I saw my beauty and not the ugly black thing that Mom and my sisters had tried to stamp on my head. It was a new day, and no one could ever tell me I was ugly. Each day I woke up, it brought new strength and determination. Watch out…this girl is on fire. I knew one day I could use my looks to get what I wanted in life. I knew I would never be the same again. I knew with God; all things are possible. During that time, with all my ups and downs, peace was still hard to find.

The wedding took place as planned. Mom and Joe were happy and drinking. The preacher was getting drunk in the kitchen with the men. The music started to play, and it was a blues song. My thought was how ironic for a blues song to be playing on my wedding day. Little did I know, that was the start of a new kind of blues for me. Everybody was at the house that I would be calling home. My husband's brother, Roy, lived there, too. Joe and Roy shared a bedroom, and I thought, after our wedding night, this will be me and Joe's room.

After everyone had gotten drunk and gone home, it was time for us to go to sleep. Roy had fallen asleep in the room that I thought was mine and my husband's. I begged my husband to wake him up and put him on the couch, but he said Roy was too drunk to wake up, and we will take care of business and fix things with Roy the next day. So, believe it or not, I spent my wedding night, in a bedroom with twin beds, and with Joe's brother. A new awakening for me, who in the hell lets their bride sleep in the same room with a drunk brother? Till this day, I think Roy was awake, checking out his baby brother and his wife. Some sick stuff. It wasn't long before they both were snoring. Joe's two to three-minute ride was over, and I was left thinking, *"What was that?"* Did he think this was for both of us? Did he not remember it was our wedding night, and it should be something special? No, he didn't give it a thought. Over the course of the next three years, our marriage lacked in many ways. I don't really know if he understood me, and wanted to fulfil my needs, but according to him, I was the blame for our failed marriage.

I was pretty sure Mom wanted to be free of us all and I was right. The next morning after my wedding, I got a message to go see Mom off at the bus station that evening. I didn't think she would be leaving the next day. I was surprised since she never said to me that she was going to

Detroit the very next day. I think Joe knew but was told not to tell me. He probably helped with her ticket. She sold me out again, married me off one day, and was getting out of town the next day. Here comes that hurt again. My world was falling apart again, left on my own with this man nine years older than me. It was kind of like being left with a father figure. I liked my husband a lot, but love was nowhere near, and Joe wasn't trying to introduce me to any art of love. I didn't even know what love was, and the way he was treating me, I knew I would not be falling in love with him no time soon. I tried to talk with Joe to let him know that when we had sex he was not including me. It was just sex. We were not making love.

"You don't include me, you ride me and then take your sorry butt to sleep," I told him. Even with my young age, I knew I needed intimacy and love making. Hearing my friends talk about going to new heights and hearing bell rings, was not happening. The only noise I was hearing was heavy breathing for a few minutes and the snoring would began. I started wondering if there was something wrong with me. We didn't have too much in common, he was a hard worker and wanted me to be a hard-working housewife. I was used to all of that, even taking care of my children was easy. I was fifteen when my first child was born and turned sixteen a few months after that. I had a very hard labor, and then Joe, Jr. made his entrance into the world. I was so glad to get that eight pounds oversized kid out of me. I thought I was going to die. Joe was very proud of his son, looking just like him. Mom was happy she had a grandson. Joe, Jr. was the first boy in our family. Before him, it was only girls.

After Mom went to Detroit, I helped by sending her care packages. Joe would get upset because money was missing, but I didn't care. I felt I had to help my Mom and sisters. One would think by now, I could care less about my Mom and sisters because of the way I was treated. However, but I knew I would always love her and my sisters.

Chapter Seven

JOE'S TRUE COLORS

Joe would slap me at the drop of a hat, when I would say something that was offensive or set him off. I knew I could slice like a knife with my words. I still cursed a lot, and when he made me mad, I would cuss him out. Perhaps he thought he was a disciplinarian more than a husband. You would think that because he was much older, he would have been trying to teach me something, but that never happened. He and Mom both knew, I didn't know anything about being a wife and neither one of them tried to teach or help me. When I was eight months pregnant, I said something, and he slapped me so hard he gave me a big black eye. Mom had slapped me many times but never gave me a black eye. I don't remember him ever saying he was sorry.

After my son was born, things were as well as to be expected. Looking from the outside you would see a lovely family, a husband working hard, coming home to his wife, and child. But on the inside, I was crying. I loved my son, and it seemed to me he was a different kind of child, like my sisters. Joe, Jr. cried all the time, if he wasn't feed on the scheduled time, he would yell and if I didn't hold him, he would cry all night. I didn't know was going on with my son. His attitude was hard to describe.

Joe loved his son but thought it was the wife's duty to always take care of him. I had no help from him. During the second year of marriage, I got pregnant with my baby girl, Bridgitte. She was a beautiful baby and wasn't a crier. She had the sweetest smile and was always happy. I didn't understand any of this, my son made me think I never wanted another child but when she came, I knew I could handle another one. Bridgitte was precious and at an early age, I discovered she had a mind of her own. She walked at eight months and was good at it. I loved and enjoyed my children; they were my life. My children gave me joy. My son was a lot like his father, but he was cute and a bundle of joy. I know now, without them I couldn't have made it for three years with their father.

I wanted to go somewhere, do something. My husband was a couch potato never wanting to go anywhere but to the country to see his parents, back home, and to work. I was going crazy. I kept asking Joe if I could go to my school prom with a few friends just to get out for a while. He finally said yes. I went to the prom and saw old friends and regretted that I didn't get a chance to be a part of my graduating class. We went to breakfast after prom was over, and I admit, I missed not being able to finish school. I truly enjoyed being out with people my age.

When I got home, my husband was waiting behind the door, and he slapped me as I came in saying, "You should have been home." I tried to explain, but he didn't hear any of it. At that very moment, I knew I would never let him hit me again. I made up my mind that one day I would leave him. I wanted my children to have a father and never wanted them to be like me. I never knew what a father was until the Lord let me know that I had a father who would always be there for me in Him. So, believing that the Lord would be their father, I knew I couldn't stay. I couldn't live that way.

After that slap, I didn't like him anymore, and I lost respect for him. I thought that chapter of my life would be closed one day. I didn't know how, but I knew I would never continue to stay and be used as a piece of meat and beaten nightly. I didn't want to be the person he could hit on when he felt like letting off some steam. I had to walk that thin line and do everything he thought I should. If he thought beating was a way to get me in order, well my dear, that little brown girl was not putting up with it anymore.

I wanted to take my two beautiful children to Detroit to see Mom and my sisters. I made the trip before when my son was a year old. Joe knew Mom wanted to see her grandson, the first boy in the family. That time he agreed to let me go. This time, I had to try to get him to let me go so she could see Bridgitte. He put up a fight but finally said yes. I said, "Now I could get away from him and see my Mom and sisters." I was so excited because they were the only family that I could call my own. Marie and her husband had left Memphis shortly after I got married and was living in New Orleans. After all my family had moved, I felt I was alone and by myself even while being with Joe. I thought that I could spend a little time with my family. Although they weren't the greatest, they were all I had.

The trip was two long days and a night by bus, but it was so worth it. Getting away from the boring lifestyle and walking on eggshells while being raped at night if I didn't give it up was too much. Joe thought I was his to have whenever he wanted it, and it didn't matter how I felt, or whether I said no. He forced himself on me after a couple of weeks after giving birth; he should have waited six weeks. He didn't care. It would be a time to get a break for ten days, and it was my plan. The trip was awesome despite the long hours and restless night. It was better than being home. By the time we got there, it was beautiful. I'm reasonably sure Mom was happy having us there. She loved Joe Jr., and it was a blessing for her. She enjoyed Bridgitte, too, and spent time with her, however, she let us know that Joe Jr. was her favorite. It was okay because my sisters made a big deal with Bridgitte. They had a baby girl to play with, and Bridgitte received plenty of love.

We were there two days before Mom went to the hospital. She had a liver disease and would have to stay for a while. In the meantime, I met her neighbors, Pat and Ronnie. They were singers, and one of the guys that sang with them was Joe Harris. Their group was the Fabulous Peps.

I transformed into another world from that scene. Joe and I started making eye contact the moment we met. He loved my eyes, and I enjoyed him singing to me. We started hanging out right away. I would visit Mom during the day, and he would take me to the spots where they were performing at night, mostly on the weekends. He would sing to me, and I thought I would lose my mind.

The songs were excellent, and thousands of people were screaming and going wild when they performed. I had the best seat in the house and Joe would sing to me while the spotlight was on me. I knew this was something out of a fairy tale and I was the princess. After the show, he would take me to dinner with the little money they had made from the weekend gig and introduced me to Chinese food and I loved it. It was all happening on the weekend, and I was enjoying myself for a change. Mom was still in the hospital, and my husband was demanding me to come home after a couple of weeks. I told him I couldn't leave with my Mom in the hospital and leave my sisters by themselves. I didn't tell him we had cousins a few doors away and they helped me by babysitting. Nothing was stopping me, nothing this grand had ever happen with, or to me, and I loved it. My husband was threatening and demanding by the third week. I paid him no mind. I didn't give a care about him and his demanding lifestyles. I continue enjoying my new life. I was in love for the first time. I had two children and never had reached the height of lovemaking as I had with Joe Harris. I felt it for the first time. I sat up laughing and thought, this is what my friends were talking about when they said they were climbing the walls and hearing bells ring when they were making love. I understood.

Joe Harris was loving, kind, and gentle with me and it wasn't long before I loved me some little Joe. He was in love, too. We spent every night together, and I woke up to him looking into my eyes every morning. He always said how pretty my eyes were. He was mesmerized staring at me, and I was mesmerized by his presence and his singing. He was so gifted with a voice that could captivate not just me, but thousands. I knew it was going to be the saddest day of my life when it was time to go home and leave this fairy tale. The fourth week was coming up, and by that time my husband was out-right threatening to hurt me and demanding that I bring his children home. Again, I would give him the report about Mom, not that he cared, he just wanted me back. Joe couldn't ride alone, he was missing this body to jump on and ride every night. I am sure he loved his kids, but I couldn't stay for the kids anymore.

Before meeting Joe Harris, I had already seen the good, bad, and ugly. I had already made up my mind that I would not be staying. It just made it easier for me. I continue my new life putting my old one on hold for as long as I could, spending time with my Mom. I spent time with family in the day, my new friends, the Peps, and making love with Joe all night. The thought of us having to say good-bye soon made us draw closer and cling to one another. Our love grew stronger each passing day. We loved so hard and couldn't seem to get enough of each other. We were behaving as if it was our last day on this earth.

Mom ended up staying in the hospital for six weeks, and while there, she tried to convince me to go home to my husband. She assured me that my cousin could take care of my sisters. I wasn't staying for my sisters. I was staying for myself. I was in love with my prince who rescued me from the hell and heartache I was experiencing. He showed me what love was all about. I was in love with a life I'd never known could be so wonderful. I was happy during that time, and I wanted more of it. I wanted it to last forever. However, nothing wonderful lasts forever for me. It was time for Mom to leave the hospital and I was preparing to bring her home, and I would be on the bus the next day to go home.

For both, Joe and I, our last night together was brutal. We held each other and loved so hard because we didn't know what was next. We didn't know if we would be together again. Even if we did, we wondered if it would ever be as good as it had been during those six weeks. Mom was home, and as Joe and I said our goodbyes, I was numb. Ironically, for the first time, I wasn't sad about leaving my family, but my heart was aching having to say goodbye to my prince.

Going to the bus station was a hard pill to swallow. The pain was coming again. it was like riding a horrible roller coaster. I hadn't prepared for it, and my fairy tale was coming to an end. I saw the raw hurt in his eyes, and he was feeling the pain, too. To make the situation unbearable, before I left, Walter Jackson started to sing, "Any day now, you will hear me say, good-bye my love, and you will be on your way." It broke us down. We held on to each other for dear life at the station, hearing all aboard tore us apart for the last time. The kids and I boarded and saw him standing there until the bus left the station, my heart was crying. While I was trying to be strong for my children, but the hurt was real and stronger than ever. My children needed my attention, and I thanked God for them. As bad as my heart was hurting, my children would feel the worst of it, so I had to love them and give the tender love and care they needed. I had to store the tears up until they went to sleep and when they did, I cried all that night. My world had fallen apart, and I was on my way back to the worse kind of treatment. I questioned, *"Does it ever end?"*

I arrived home, and I knew my husband was glad, not to mention he was waiting for an opportunity to slap me again for something. It didn't have to be a big deal. He just wanted to do it. I walked very carefully, knowing I could end up with a black eye or messed up face.

I was home for a couple of months and realized that my period hadn't come. I knew right away that I was pregnant, and I knew it was not my husband's. I went to the doctor and he confirmed it. I knew I had to come up with a plan and I put one in motion. I knew for sure I couldn't stay because my husband would know it wasn't his child. My life would be hell. He had already threatened to put me in my place, whatever place he thought that was. He tried to slap me one day, and I fell on the bed. He was over me telling me to get up, and with a relaxed piece of mind I said, "Not this time, buddy." One of my brothers-in-law, Johnnie, was pulling him away telling him to leave his sister-in-law alone. He was pleading with him not to hit me anymore. Most of my in-laws loved me even my father-in-law. The only one who didn't love me was his oldest sister. She was like the wicked witch of the West.

During the six weeks I was in Detroit, she had moved in and sowed bitter seeds about me to my husband, and he was eating it all up. I didn't stand a chance. As I lay on that bed while he was telling me to get up, I was mapping out a plan to leave in my mind. I held on to the thought that, any day I would be on my way. Once I make the plan and know the path I must take, I put it into action. I remembered something Pastor Linda, my pastor, said one day, "Vision before the Victory."

Tiring of him telling me to get up, I finally sat up. When I did, I knew what I would do to get away from him. I had a good friend that drove a limousine. I called my friend the next day and asked if he could pick me up and take me to the other side of town where "the Giant" lived. I had not spoken to "the Giant" since the day I left, and somehow, I knew where he was, although I still can't remember how I knew. My friend agreed to pick me up the next morning. He wasn't a close friend of the family, but he knew most of them. My last night with my husband was a good night for him, and it was okay for me knowing this would be his last ride, so I said to myself, *"Make it good baby, you will remember this night for a long-time because I am out of here."* The next morning, he was off to work, and I did him a courtesy. I wrote him a note on the wall saying, "Sorry we were not able to make it." It was as simple as that. I packed a few things liked clothes, my iron, and clock. I had my two children and was pregnant with the third. I knew when I hit Detroit that I had to work.

My friend, Franklin, was a driver for the owners of one of the most prestigious hotels in Memphis. When he picked me up in the limo, all eyes were on me as I was making my exit. I always managed to make a statement in whatever situation I was encountering. We didn't have limos pulling up in the projects in the sixties. I indeed was the talk of "Peyton Place" aka the projects. My friend got out, opened the door for my children and I, then he got in the driver's seat and asked, "Where to?" I said to myself *I like this,* and I knew I wanted more of that kind of service. I was so grateful to be getting away. I looked back one last time and never thought about it again. I found out later that my friend was in love with me and that's why he took the chance to help me. He had shared that with one of the twins, a small world I'd say. I had no idea because I had a crush on his best friend who I had met during one of the Yancey's party a few years back.

We arrived at "the Giant's" house, and I got out telling Franklin I would knock on the door and be right back. The door opened, and there he stood. We looked at each other for a few minutes, and I said, "I have left my husband, I need a place to stay until 7:00 pm, when the bus travels from Memphis to Detroit, and I need some money. Will you help me?" He said yes and when he walked out of the house and saw the limo and driver, he and my Stepmom looked as if they had seen a ghost. They couldn't speak. I introduced my friend and let "the Giant" know he was helping me. My Stepmom grabbed the kids, and "the Giant" took my box and bag in the house, so I could say goodbye to my friend. I thanked him, and he placed thirty dollars in my hand and said he wished he could have given me more. We hugged, wished each other well, and he got in the limo, and that was the last time I saw the man that loved me enough to take the hit to help me. There was always an angel nearby to help me.

"The Giant" seemed to enjoy my children, while my Stepmom was calling them their grandchildren. I didn't care. I just wanted 7:00 pm to come so I could ride away and never look back. They gave me a suitcase so I could get rid of the box and bag, put some money in my hands, and took us to the bus station that evening. I hugged them, pausing longer to embrace my Stepmom more to let her know I valued and appreciated her. We didn't mention a word about what happened in the past. It is easier to leave angry words unspoken than to mend hearts that were broken. From that moment on, I knew he had forgiven me, and I was okay with that. It still hurts to think of what he did to my sister, but he was trying, and he had to live with that. That was between him and God. For me to harbor bitterness would cause my happiness to dock somewhere else. I needed to be happy and at peace for what I was doing and the road ahead I had to travel. I knew a heavy load lifted off both of our shoulders. He didn't know what to make of Willie Frances, the little brown girl who defied him in every area. I demanded respect, and he had to give it up.

Chapter Eight

DETROIT:
MY THIRD AND FINAL TRIP

The bus pulled out from the station and merged into traffic, and I was leaving Memphis with each mile. I never looked back and I didn't allow my mind to think of how it would affect my husband coming home to an empty and quiet home. There would be no children's laughter and no wife waiting to run his bath water. I imagine it would be the worst day of his life, yet I never thought of it until now. I had to take time to repent and ask God to forgive me for taking the children from him. I saw that day coming because my mind was made up long before it happened. Some of his family said I left him for another man. It was not the truth. If I had not met Joe Harris, I would have still left my husband eventually. The situation gave me a way out a little sooner. My freedom was right around the corner or, so I thought.

When I arrived in Detroit, Mom was doing one of her numbers, acting as though she was surprised to see us. At first glance, it appeared she had a thought in her mind. I couldn't exactly say what she was thinking, maybe she was mad at me for leaving. After a few days, the truth surfaced; she stated I should go back to my husband. She kept saying she couldn't take care of my kids and me. Joe Harris had gone to Ohio and was singing with the group called The Ohio Players. He didn't know I was coming nor did he know that I was pregnant. I told Mom I could work up until my baby was born, take off for a couple of weeks and would find a job again. She didn't want to hear my plan, she started nitpicking about any and everything.

During one of her nitpicking times, I argued back at her and she put my babies and me out in the snow and would not open the door. We sat on the porch as the snow continued to come down. My children were hungry, so I went to the little neighborhood store and told the owner that we were hungry. I offered to pay him back if he would let me get bread, lunch meat, and milk for my children. He told me to get what I needed. I knew it was God making a way for me. He was always there to help me along the way. He said He would never leave or forsake me, and If I acknowledge Him, He would direct my path. Even in my misery, I never felt alone. I paid the owner of the store back a month later, and he looked me in the eyes and assured me he would always be there for me. He didn't know me at all. He had only seen me a couple of times. God sends the angel to open hearts of those who will help you. That's God.

We had cousins living nearby. I didn't want anybody to know Mom's actions, but I had to tell the truth. The chick had put me out. I was pregnant and with my babies, her grandchildren, wow! That hit me like a ton of bricks. My cousin had ten children, there were babies everywhere, but I needed to lay my head down and think. I knew I was equipped with greatness. God had seen to that. I was the sole caregiver for my children, and I had to make sure they didn't feel too much of the craziness. My cousins, Rose and Fordie, allowed me to stay with them for a few days until I could go to see if my Mom would let me come back until I had the baby, got a job, and out of her house. When she realized I wasn't going back to Memphis, she accepted it, and softened up a little. I was glad because I was also penniless.

To get public assistance, during those times, a person had to be a resident of Detroit for a year before they could even get food stamps. I tried to get help from my husband rather than be forced to take him to court.

He wouldn't send me a dime. Mom was in a rough section of Detroit, and there were many rackets to make a few dollars. I was as country as a brown egg and had to learn fast. Otherwise, the bright lights and big city would have swallowed me up. I got a job working at a small restaurant and Mom was happy that I was bringing money home, so she could have a few dollars and, rightfully so. Unfortunately, it wasn't long before the boss had to let me go. He wasn't making enough to keep me on the pay-roll. So, out in the cold again I went. I made a crazy and desperate move that paid off.

I had two male friends I used to kick it with. They were going to Idlewild, Michigan. It was the place to be during hunting season. Idlewild is located 250 miles North of Detroit and 300 miles Northwest of Chicago, Illinois. During the first half of the 20th century, it was one of the few resorts in the country where African Americans were allowed to vacation and purchase property, before such discrimination became illegal in 1964. It surrounds Lake Idlewild, and the headwaters of the Pere Marqueete River run through the area. (Source: www.michigan.org) There was a lot of action happening there during that time. They were telling me that we could make money if I went as well. I was five months pregnant by that time but still not showing. They also said I could get a job being a waitress.

I saw it as an opportunity to make some money and provide a good Christmas for my children. Picture this, two black guys and a female on the road hitchhiking to Idlewild from Detroit. We would have to go through 250 miles of rough weather and snow to get there, and all I had to eat was a bowl of beans that I brought with me. God sent His mercy all the same. We started off with a couple of rides then we had to walk some. It was getting dark and we didn't know what we would do and we had not thought the trip out that far. Then God sent an angel, a kind Caucasian guy who was shocked that we were going that far by way of thumb. He said the only reason he picked us up was because of me. He said he just had to help, so he took us to his house, fed us a good warm meal, and put us up for the night. He allowed me to sleep in his bedroom and he and the guys slept in the front room. Look at my God.

The next morning, he fed us breakfast and took us to the outskirts of town, so it would be easier to get a ride. All the people that gave us rides were white guys. Some were just curious, and some just wanted to help three crazy kids get to where they needed to go. We got a few more rides, and we made it. Fortunately, we were able to pay for our hotel when we checked out. It was a blessing. Because of the time of the year, the businesses were gearing up to make big money. I started working as a waitress, and after a few days, I met another waitress, Kelly, who seemed to be a very nice girl. She had an extra room and allowed me to rent it which was cheaper than the hotel. I separated from the guys and moved in with my new friend and her mother. Once I separated from the guys I never saw them again. I knew that God had sent another angel to help me. My friend and her mother welcomed me into their home and cared for me.

Things were looking good for a few weeks, and then I got sick with a bad cold and the flu. I tried working but I was too sick. I ended up meeting a couple who had come to Idlewild to party. When they were ready to go home, they saw how sick I was and offered to take me all the way back to Detroit. I had hitched all the way to Idlewild and was driven all the way back in style in the couple's beautiful Lincoln Continental. Again, I was thinking, *look at God.* He said, "I will never leave you or forsake you." I had saved money from working before I got sick. Kelly and her Mom wouldn't take any money for rent so I was able to bring all that I had made back home.

We had a beautiful Christmas and enough food to last during my sick time. After the new year rolled in and out, Joe came home from Ohio and found out what I had done. He was mad as hell and kept asking me how I could have taken a chance with that trip to Idlewild. I explained to him that he was unable to help me, and he wasn't making enough to buy our Christmas dinner, and for sure he wasn't able to buy toys for my children. I explained that I understood it was hard times and that I didn't blame him for not being able to help me. The next thing I knew, he was off to Ohio again, and I was left doing my last months of pregnancy alone. I think I saw him one time after that.

I started working in the "single action numbers" which were an illegal, big-time numbers' running rack in the East. Each time, the first number was out, my job was to pick up bets from five places. There was a time restraint on it, so I had to get back to the place in a certain amount of time to put the second bet in for the next number until six numbers were called. The task was to get it all done within three hours. If someone won, you would have to pay the bet off and move on to the next stop. The cops were riding four deep, which we called the "Big 4." These cops were vicious. They would stop me, trying to find out exactly what I was up to and why I was there. My response was always the same lie, "going to the store." The cops knew I was lying and they always gave me a break. When God is for you, who can be against you? I really think my angels were guiding me every step of the way, and when danger would come near, they would protect me.

After a while, when the "Big 4" would see me, they would shout out the window, "get your butt off the streets." As I got further along in my eighth month, the "Big 4" would tell me I was going to have the baby in the snow. I would just say, "I need to go to the store." As for everyone else, they took them to jail. They beat up so many heads and treated the prostitutes really bad, calling them awful names. By the grace and mercy of God that was keeping me, it was nothing they could say or do to me. They always just left me alone. I worked till I was eight and half months, and by that time, Mom had moved us to an old monstrous looking house near a slaughterhouse. She said, "We will need more room for the baby." She was trying, I think, one just never knew with her.

Every morning I could hear the slaughtering of the hogs, and that just about drove me crazy. I had met an ambulance driver, Kenobi Keona Cassahalia, who was from Nigeria and was enrolled in college. Kenobi was black as night. The only thing you could see was the white on his collar at night. Kenobi was another Godsend. I was anemic, and the doctor told me I needed plenty of spinach and liver. He would make sure I had those things and Mom would make sure I was taken care of by cooking my meals. I didn't know what to make of this because it was a new side of her. I am sure she knew I was about to have the baby, then go back to work, and she would have money again.

Kenobi was the only friend I had in those last few weeks of my pregnancy. I thank God for Kenobi, especially since he took me to my last doctor appointment. The doctor informed me that things were well. I believed my checkup went well because of the spinach and liver I had eaten. Shortly after the checkup, Phaedra, my baby girl was on her way. It was about 3:00 a.m. when Mom went next door and called for the ambulance. Kenobi was waiting for the call. He was there in no time and got me to the hospital fast. I would shout out, "Slow this damn thing down," but he kept moving. When we arrived at the hospital, I was rushed in and I had the baby while Mom was still admitting me.

The baby came in less than an hour. I think Kenobi scared her out of my womb with his driving. What a blessing. She was a beautiful and healthy. I was concerned because with my other son and daughter, I had stayed in labor for over twenty hours. With all the hell I'd been through, I just didn't know. She was so adorable. The doctors kept assuring me she was just fine.

The next day, the nurse came into the room and announced that my "husband" Mr. Yancy, was there to see me. I didn't quite know what to expect, and in comes Kenobi. I just said hello Mr. Yancey. He was so kind, he brought me flowers and helped me pick out a name for my beautiful baby girl. Kenobi came up with the name, Phaedra, and the way he said it, with his accent, sounded so good. I agreed with the name right away. He said he would be leaving in a few days, heading back to college. His angel assignment was complete. He made sure he was there when I was released. When he got me home safely, and he was out of my life just as fast as he entered it. Thank you, Father, for my angel. Thank you, Father, for never leaving me.

Three weeks later, I was working at Fort Wayne Army Base. Getting up at five in the morning and taking three buses in the snow. I was happy. I had a real job, but I also knew I was merely passing through. God had something else better for me. I met and began dating Jim, who was a Captain. Jim was kind and seemed very interested and happy to date me.

My boss at the Base, was a fat, Caucasian slob who was always making advances at me. He was just nasty looking, so I knew my time was limited and I would have to get the heck out of there before something bad would happen. My boss would call me into his office and try to make me have sex with him. He even had the nerve to put plastic on his penis, so I wouldn't be near his skin. I was mortified about the fat greasy, red, ugly bastard trying to take advantage of a poor young worker I told him hell no and that what he wanted me to do would never happen. I was seriously making plans for my exit. There had to be a better way.

Joe finally came to see his daughter. She was six weeks old. He came with milk and diapers and I thought that was nice of him, but I wasn't impressed. So, I asked him to go for a walk with me. I knew he thought we would pick up where we left off but that just didn't do it for me. I had been beaten up so bad and alone by myself for so long. I wasn't feeling him. I put it out there and told him it is over. This chapter is closed. He was pissed. He said, "Ain't no woman ever quit me." I said, "OK...It's all good, let me be the first." I told him I was ready to tear Detroit up, get plenty of money, and bring my babies and family out of the rat-infested ugly building, which we have been forced to live in. I told him that I would never live like that again. In my heart, I knew I had to see it before I could achieve it. I had visualized the good life, and I wanted it. My thoughts were that we couldn't continue. Love requires sacrifice and time apart makes people strangers with the ones they love. We could never make it like it was. Life would not allow it. So, like a song says, "He would only be in my way."

He didn't take it very well, but we were able to hang out a few times after that. He just didn't have any hold on me and I believed we would always be friends. I will always love him. We had the chance of a lifetime to love and be loved in such a beautiful way. However, what we did have was the lovely gift Phaedra, the daughter we both loved dearly. He is the father of my daughter, and he lets me know it every Mother's Day with a lovely phone call. Over the years, I looked forward to it. He is proud of the beautiful and gifted child we made together. She is truly our love child. She has the best of each of us. Love, compassion, dedication, commitment, and a passion for life.

Three weeks later, we moved out of the ugly house into a nice two-bedroom apartment. That was Mom's apartment. A month later, we had our own place. I was on a roll. I was still working for the army base, and dating Jim, who was good to me and loved to spoil me. I really could've cleaned up hustling army men, but I was happy just being with Jim, he didn't mind giving up the money.

By the time I had moved and was steady in a relationship with Jim, I was eligible for help from the county around that same time. I had been invited to a house party, and it was my first introduction to such events. I saw the house parties as an opportunity to make money, so I had my first party a few weeks later and I incorporated gambling tables and made over three hundred dollars the first time. When I made my first appearance at the county building, I had that money in my purse.

I had another party about three weeks later, and that one was better than the first. I had a crap table in the bedroom, a card table in the living room, and I had a cook frying chicken and selling dinners in the kitchen. While we were partying, a knock came on the door and low and behold, it was my first house call from the county social worker. Mr. Brown, was a young, tall, handsome, serious-looking, Caucasian man. He stepped in the house and snapped his head from side to side as he scanned my place. I could tell he was thinking something, I reacted and quickly made up a story in hopes of getting his mind off his thoughts.

Mr. Brown said to me he was going to be my assigned social worker and these activities in my house would not look good on the report he was required to file to his superiors. Praise God, it is not what man says, but what God says. Give thanks in all things. Nothing could stop me from doing what I had to do, and that was to make money and give my family what we needed. I vowed that my children would never go hungry, or wear rags for clothes like me, and they never did.

After the house parties thinned out, I decided to get a job at the famous Twenty Grand as a waitress. I was introduced to the number one spot in Detroit. It was home to many famous singers. The Fabulous Peps which was Little Joe's group, and Martha Jean, the Queen who loved her some Little Joe Harris. She was mistress of ceremony at the club as well as a famous radio announcer in the days of Marvin Gaye, Gladys Knight and the Pips, the Spinners, and the Temptations. I worked there for six magical months however the building I lived in was not-so magical. It became very apparent that I needed to move, especially after I stabbed a woman's husband. I couldn't raise my kids in that kind of environment.

One night before leaving, my friends and I was at a party. Some big dark fellows picked a fight with Jim. They harassed him for being light-skinned. One of the fellows called Jim the little red dude, and Jim got pissed and said something back. The guy grabbed him, body slammed him onto a car, and punched him. I pulled my four-inch switchblade out and stabbed him four times. When I realized what I had done, blood was everywhere. His wife was trying to beat me up, and I said to her, "while you are trying to hurt me, your husband is bleeding to death so stop the dumb stuff." He was rushed to the hospital and treated. The doctors said the wounds were to the upper part of his shoulder. No extensive damage was done. I praised the Lord. After that, I didn't feel safe anymore and Jim orders came in to go overseas. His ship would be sailing out. Again, I was alone. It was time to go, time to get out. I moved from the West side of town to the East side.

Chapter Nine

MOM'S DEPARTURE, MY GUILT

Mom's health was declining. Her favorite food was pork, especially pork sausages or bacon. She was addicted to pork of any kind. Mom loved the pig. Every time she would eat it, her blood pressure would hit the ceiling, but she wouldn't stop. The doctor told her if she continued to eat pork, her blood pressure would go up so high they wouldn't be able to bring it down. And that's just what happened. Mom had a stroke.

She was mad at me because I wouldn't bring her pork sausages to the hospital. She threatened me if I didn't show up with the sausages, the next time I see her, she would be dead. I decided not to take the pork sausages, and I got a call saying we had better come back to the hospital, as Mom was checking out. By the time we made it she had passed away.

I was so angry with her. Mom had been hurting me all my life, and had never been the mother that I longed for, wished for, or needed. Now she was gone. I felt that she had put a guilt on me that I had to live with for the rest of my life. I couldn't tell anybody what she had said to me, not even my sisters. I felt if I had just taken the sausage, she would be alive. It was the hardest thing to say no to the sausage. Having guilt and not knowing how to deal with it stripped me of my dreams and my ambitions.

Aunt Marie picked us up from the hospital took us to her house to comfort and talk things over. She made coffee and pulled out her stash of gin. She told us to pour some in our coffee to make us feel better. To me, hot coffee with gin just didn't sound good. It wasn't. However, it did knock off the rough edges and calmed us down a little. After that day, I drank every day while trying to take care of everything and everybody.

I learned the value of friendship during that season, though. Before Mom's passing, I moved to the East side of town and met my dear friend, Gladys. She introduced me to Jerome who I dated for a few weeks. We were new in our relationship, but I liked him a lot. Later, I fell in love with him. He and Gladys were a blessing in helping me raise money for the funeral arrangements. That's when I realized the importance of friends. I had a new kind of respect for Gladys. She jumped right in and started organizing and putting the house in order, so when friends started dropping by with gifts of love and money, they wouldn't walk into a mess. Folks could never say our house wasn't presentable. I thank God that I had a real friend that carried me in times of trouble. I was genuinely grateful for the help and support. I was able to put Mom away in the right way because of Gladys, Jerome, and some others. Without them, things would have been very different. The county wanted to put her away in a field where they put people that didn't have insurance or didn't have the money to buy a grave site. They also offered a wooden box, which I felt she deserved, but I was better than that. I had to see it done right and I did.

During this time both of my younger sisters were pregnant, and Marie was just there. She tried, but I could tell my sisters did not give a damn. They needed outfits for the service, and I had to find a size fifty-two dress for my Mom. By the grace of God. I found a $750.00 yellow, raw silk dress with beautiful sequins and pearls. It was all the Lord and His angels leading me to this shop in an upscale area of Detroit. I can't remember how, or what I was doing there. I had looked everywhere to find a dress for this woman. I was led to go in this little shop. I felt out of place just stepping in, and the owner knew I was out of my league. She asked in her way, not nasty, but like, "what could she possibly do for me?" I told her my situation, and she hesitated for a minute, then her face lit up, and she said, "follow me." We went to the back of the shop, and she brought out the beautiful dress. She said a lady had custom-ordered it and never came to pick it up. I told her it was no way I could afford anything like that. She asked how much money I had. I told her only $75.00. She said it would be a blessing, to let me have it. I was in tears knowing it was God. He led me to that shop and the amazing owner. She was happy to be a help and a blessing to me.

I took the dress back to the mortuary, and it was the talk of the place. Everyone thought my Mom was a famous person being put away in dress made with raw silk, sequins, and pearls. She looked beautiful, looking better dead than alive, sad to say. I thanked God for all He had done for me and my family. When I finished with my Mom, I went to work on my three sister's outfits for the service. It was customary for people to wear black to funerals. I had my black dress and I was okay. I just needed to put the finances together to pay for their dresses. Money was coming in from all over. It was indeed a blessing seeing friends and relatives come together to help me. I learned the value of friends that I hold true today. *Friends fill the void where family avoids.* I love my friends and thank God for blessing me with so many. I am blessed. Proverb 17.17 says, "A friend loves at all times." It also states that a friend sticks closer than a brother. In my walks in life, my friends have been closer to me, than my Mom and sisters. They didn't know how to give love, only to receive it.

The morning of the funeral. I was locked in the bathroom drinking scotch. Jerome was at the door begging me to come out. I did not want to see her. I didn't want to ride in the family car following the hearse. I put the bottle in my purse, knowing I would need it later. I hadn't cried yet because the guilt and anger wouldn't let me. It was killing me, and I couldn't tell anyone, not even my sisters. I felt if I didn't repeat what she had said the night she died, it wouldn't be real. If I didn't talk about it, it would go away. Little did I know, holding it and drinking the alcohol would rob me of many of my dreams. It would take years for me to recover.

The service went well and the repass was at Aunt Marie's home. I was blessed enough to find a gravesite right next to my praying Aunt Ada. The one who was always fussing at Mom, when we were babies and telling her to take better care of us. Then Mom stopped taking us around her. How ironic to lay her right beside the one who tried so hard to help her. I had peace knowing she was close to Aunt Ada. It was easy for me to allow my mind to slip away and remember when she used to play with us. Remembering her bathing us, kissing our little feet, telling us how much she loved us. She was a beautiful spirit. A praying woman, and now they lie, side by side.

At the repast, was the first day I had a decent meal since that horrible night. It was the first day that I saw the sun. It was there all along, but everything was black to me at the beginning of her end. I felt better when they lowered that casket into the ground. A heavyweight lifted off me. I could finally say, "It is over, you can never hurt me again." She couldn't, but I didn't think about how I could hurt myself. I drank and cried in my alcohol, for many years. Every Mother's Day, I would cry, and condemn myself and just allow the guilt to eat me. I took my children's Mother's Day happiness away, crying over the past, over a woman that didn't take the time to care. She didn't deserve any of my tears. That emotional stress dulled my dreams and devalued me.

I was still taking care of family, my sisters, plus their children. I believe I would have been more productive, a better mother, and made better choices if I wasn't taking care of everybody. I was a periodic drinker, but it was still a lot. When I felt like it had gotten to be too much, I would check out from life and visit my dreams. I was always a dreamer. If I could see it, I could achieve it when I was not on a drinking binge. Most things were in order. We had food and all the necessities. Bridgitte was old enough to take care of business. She was so much like me. Her maternal instincts would just kick in. She was my daughter, my best friend, and the next one in charge in my drinking "absences." She knew how to take care of business at a young age, and she took care of me, too. I used alcohol as an excuse. I didn't have to think. I didn't have to worry and care for everybody.

Now, my sisters, they were no joke when it came to drinking alcohol. Two of them were alcoholics, like myself, and Pearl the youngest, was one short of a six-pack. That chick was a professed crazy woman. She would tell us she was mental, so if I do some crazy stuff don't be surprised...I warned you. She didn't lie. I lived in denial for many years hoping that she wasn't all the way out there. I was praying that she would get better and grow up one day. She never did. I would always talk to God, telling him I am taking care of your children and I don't want to be old when I finish this mission. I asked Him many times to renew my youth, like the eagle, to help me to be strong, and not to let this take me out. His strength and mercy always took me through.

Mom tried to marry Pearl off as soon as she found out she was pregnant. The poor baby was in for a rude awakening. I wanted to distance myself from Mom, and in doing so, Pearl got involved with an older man named Bill. Because of her sexual activity with him, Pearl got pregnant. She was in the same situation I was in—pregnant by an older man. Mom wasn't exactly a role model for relationships. It seemed as though she steered us towards marrying older ones. I guess in her mind she only cared about herself. Pearl wasn't into marrying someone she wasn't in love with. She had me begging Mom not to force her into it.

I loved Pearl and the idea of her being forced to marry someone she didn't love or plan to live with for the rest of her life, was too much pain for both of us. During this time, thought, I was in good graces with Mom, as I continued to put money in her pocket, and make sure she didn't go without the things she needed.

Eventually, we won the battle for Pearl as Mom no longer forced marriage on her. Little did I know, while trying to keep Pearl from destruction, that would backfire on me, and I would have to take care of her, and Willie, her first son. He was my baby until he was five years old. Pearl had moved out when he was a year old, because she couldn't care for him. Nonetheless, four years later, I had to give Willie back to her. My kids were on me to do so. He was a mischievous little dude. When I think about those days, I laugh out loud. My kids kept telling me that I was spending too much time with him and they needed that time from me.

My other sister, Mae, had been forced to marry her husband before Pearl was pregnant. He was way older than Mae. His name was Lawrence. He was strict and very abusive. Their marriage had gotten passed me. By the time I found out about it, the wedding was in motion. Mom was always so secretive when she was trying to make something happen. Mae was very quiet and just the opposite of the hell raiser that Pearl was. Mae had five boys with Lawrence and was very miserable most of the time. She was afraid of her husband. When he came home from work, he expected everything to be in order.

Mae was only fifteen with no cooking or parenting skills. It was all too much for her. My heart went out to Mae. It was sad. I knew she was trying, but it was all overwhelming. She looked so pitiful when I would see her eyes blacken by her husband. I would ask him to please stop hurting her, but he didn't pay me any attention. After a few years, and many sons, Laurence had heart issues and had to be hospitalized for a long time. Mae lost her mind. She was leaving the boys home by themselves. She just checked out. I would beg her to take care of them and told her I would report her to child services if she didn't.

One day, she left the boys home alone and while playing around, they set the bedroom on fire. I was led to check in on them and thank God there wasn't too much damage. I saw Mom's personality in Mae. Just like Mom, she wanted freedom by any means necessary. Lawrence was dying, the kids were a lot to handle, and she didn't seem to care. I would beg her to see him, but she chose to hang with other guys. Lawrence died, and his death had little impact on Mae as she didn't even want to go to the funeral. She was more concerned about being with her new boyfriend. Lawrence's family had to take care of the funeral arrangements.

Things had gotten so bad, to the point where she wasn't taking care of herself, children, or business. I threaten to turn her in, but as it turned out, I didn't have to. She left the boys with some drunk guy for five days, and he turned them into the police. The police took them out of the house, and by the time she came down off of her "merry go round," the boys were in foster care. She blamed me for it all because of those times I threatened to call the authorities. In her mind, she needed to blame someone. For many years, she told everyone that I had her kids taken from her.

By the time I traced the boys down and went to meet their foster parents, it was like seeing my Mom. Grace, their foster Mom, opened the door and I nearly fainted. She looked just like my Mom—same size, same color, with mingled gray hair. I kept staring at her saying, "You look just like my Mom." She had a pleasant smile as she introduced me to her husband, Henry. Their home, the environment they were now in was warm. They seemed happier than they had been in a long time. *God always gives you what you need.* Grace and I formed a bond right away. She embraced me, and it was a mother's love coming from her. It was the hug I craved as a child. "It may not come when you want it, but it does come."

I stayed in touch throughout the years, and I would run Mae down, and have her talk to the boys on the phone. I made her come at certain times, and I would take her to see them. I kept them connected. When they became teenagers and started getting in trouble, and giving Grace a hard time, she asked for my help. She asked if I could take them and try to hook them up with their mother. I said yes because I knew Grace and her husband were tired, getting older, and needed a break. By then, I was living in California. The boys, Clifford and Vincent, came to live with me.

Everybody was in California except the other sons, who were still in Detroit with an uncle. Vincent and Clifford were some bad dudes. I didn't know how bad they were until things weren't going their way. I began to see them for who they were. *Bad Boys!* Mae was bouncing from place to place, just like Mom, being a restless spirit. I was trying to get her motivated enough to get a job and a place, so she could be a mother to her boys. She wasn't even on the same page with the boys and me. They were rebelling, didn't want to go to school, and always mad. They knew that Mae was not going to have that happy home they were hoping for and that made them worse. Who did they blame? Me, of course.

One day while at work, out of the blue, my mind told me to call home. God always warns me when trouble is on the rise. I dialed home, Clifford answered, and a cold chill ran up my spine. I thought something terrible is happening. I asked, "What are you doing at home?" He didn't say anything. He just had a crazy and sinister laugh. I told him to hold on since I was working the switchboard and called Bridgitte. I said for her and Mae to get to my house quickly. I got back on the line with Clifford and said, "Why are you guys at home when you should be at school?" He had that crazy laugh again. There was something eerie about it. He laughed that way again. I put him back on hold, dialed 911, and told them someone was in my house. I informed them that I was at work and to please send a car over to investigate. I got back on the line with him, and he said, "I didn't take care of them as I had for the other children." He was talking crazy and rambling. I kept that dude on the phone until Bridgitte and Mae got there. By the time they arrived, the police were pulling up as well. When they saw what the boys were doing, they were in shock. They were vandalizing my home. Vincent and Clifford took off running when they saw the police coming. Mae caught Clifford, her youngest son, as he was going over the fence. She held him till the police came and said, "Nobody messes with my sister. She has kept all of us connected." How could they do that? Vincent managed to briefly elude them, but they caught him within a few hours. They were sent back to Grace and her husband in Detroit and my heart ached for them.

The damage to my home was minimal, and I gave thanks to God for sending His angels and warning me that danger was near. I thanked Him for dispatching the angels to protect my home before they were able to wreck it. My mind went back to the young Willie destroying the "Giant's" house the same way. *What you do comes back to you.*

Now let's get back to Detroit. I just wanted to share a little about some of the extreme issues that were on my plate while I was managing jobs, my children, and their children. It was never-ending, but somebody had to do it.

Chapter Ten

BEFORE CALIFORNIA

I had been in Detroit three years and was ready to buy my first home. I was back on the job, working, stealing, hanging with my sugar-daddies, and making money. I was taking care of business before the drinking got bad, and even after, I had to do what I had to do. There were a lot of people depending on me. My priority was to my children, Joe, Bridgitte, and Phaedra. We had many good and happy days together, just me and my kids. However, when having to share me with my family members, my kids came to resent family members because it took me away from them.

When I moved into my first home, I bought everything new. I had so much money coming in by that time with help from the County of Detroit and friend of the court which enforced my husband to pay child support. The checks should've have been going directly to the courts, but I received the first check for over three thousand dollars. I called my case worker, Mr. Brown, and told him I had received and cashed the check. He lashed out and said I shouldn't have done that. I told him that since it was made out to me I thought it was mine. I cashed it.

I knew better, but I could always tell a convincingly sad story. Mr. Brown said he would straighten things out, so I wouldn't get in trouble but not to cash another one if by chance I get one. Another one came a few months later so I rushed to the bank. I knew I could get into trouble. I did what I needed to do and dealt with the consequence. You guessed it, I called, told him another big check came. I added that my lights and gas were going to be shut off, so I had to cash it. He was furious and told me he was tired of bailing me out. He accused me of taking advantage of the system. I thought to myself, the darn system had let me go for a year walking the streets, pregnant in the snow trying to feed my children. I wanted to tell him I didn't care about the system. I told him I wouldn't cash another check if he would help this one more time. I was still getting my monthly check for the County every month. However, if they would have taken action, I would have cut off and made me pay the money back. By the grace of God, I received mercy.

I invited my boss to my housewarming party, and after eyeing my beautiful house with all new furnishings, he said, "Some of my money bought some of this new stuff." I didn't lie and answered yes. That was that.

I was a barmaid at a club in town, too. I was passing off counterfeit money everywhere I went. Where I got it from isn't important, I was on a hustling binge, and I was doing whatever I thought I needed to do to make ends meet.

There was a suspicion that I was involved with passing off counterfeit money. The FBI began to investigate and talked to my boss. My boss who was drunk most of the time told the FBI that there was no way I could be doing such a thing and I was a sweet innocent young woman with three kids, and a reliable hard worker. I got out of that.

Next, I worked at Ben's Place. It was a bigger and better place with a chance to make more money. It was the talk of Detroit, and I was going in there where all the money was, and it was right around the corner from my new house. How sweet it was.

My new home was a dream come true. Jerome and I were still together, and he was a blessing as we did things together in the house. The former homeowners had started to turn the attic into a loft, and they had everything done except the insulation and carpeting. Jerome took care of that. Pearl and her son occupied the upstairs. Things were going well, and life was good. She was in school during the day which allowed me to work at night. We had a good system. I was in love with Jerome, but our relationship got rocky when I realize that he was a player. I considered myself a square, and I became bored with the relationship. I knew he was a player from the beginning. However, he was indeed there for me when my Mom passed and excellent financial support. He nursed me back to health during my time of grief. More on him later.

As I mentioned, I was working at Ben's club, and the money was good. I started hiking the price up while I was waitressing. If my tray was fifteen dollars from the bar, when I got to the table it was twenty dollars plus a tip. I stole so much money while I was working at Ben's, he asked me to please stop ripping off his customers. I can laugh out loud about it now, but then, I did what I had to do. Any other boss would have fired me, but Ben wanted me to work for him so, I did whatever I wanted. When New Year's Eve rolled around, Ben asked me to work behind the bar. Oh, my goodness, what was he thinking? Ben was asking for a rip off! He had to know I was going to get some of his money and my paycheck.

The night was going great, and my tip jar was healthy. A fellow was sitting at the bar, and during the late part of the evening, he couldn't afford any more drinks. I felt since everyone was celebrating, and it was New Year's Eve, I kept filling his glass. I was happy, making plenty of money so what could it hurt, at least that's what I thought. After the celebration was over and getting close to closing time, the fellow asked if I could drop him off a couple of blocks down the way. I said, "No problem. Let me take care of my drawer then we can leave." He waited, and we headed to my 1967 Mustang that my Japanese sugar daddy Kenny bought me. During that time, Kenny had become more than a sugar daddy while spoiling me. He was a very close family friend. My kids loved him. He always remembered their birthdays more than their father sometimes. He was a gentleman.

While driving, the fellow whose name I can't remember, suddenly put a knife to my throat. He told me to pull over and give him the money or he would slit my throat. I went straight Hollywood on him, begging and crying real tears. My tears were real because I was scared. This fellow had seen me dump my tip jar into my purse, and he knew I had a nice piece of money. I was telling him just to let me open my purse, and I would give him the money. I begged him to get the knife away from my throat. The idiot should've known that most women in Detroit carried a gun. I put my hand in my purse and wrapped it around it's pearl handle. It was a twenty-five, semi-automatic gun that Jerome bought me. I brought it out, put it up to his head, and told him I would kill him much faster than he could get that knife back to my throat. The fellow must have gotten too relaxed to think he had the upper hand on me. I cussed him out so bad and I made him feel so ashamed of himself that he begged me not me not to shoot his sorry butt.

Somehow, he managed to get out of the car. However, I felt good to be able to protect myself and my money. My kids and I always had the best, and I was not letting anybody take it from us. There was a lot of snow on the ground it was hard for him to run or walk as he was trying to get away. I began shooting around his legs and laughed so hard watching him hop through the snow like a rabbit. As he hopped through the snow, I called out to him every choice word I could think of for him trying to rob me. I never saw that bunny coward again, but I made it my business to carry my gun close to me especially if I was walking to my car alone.

Life was good for a few years after that, but my drinking had gotten worse. I was drinking way too much. I still had my Japanese friend, Kenny, and Jerome in my life. I knew Jerome's lifestyle and that he had woman boosting and hustling for him. I was what we called his square lady; I didn't have to give him money as the other women did. He wanted me for his love. He said the other women didn't mean anything special to him, that he loved me. This arrangement took a toll on me even though I knew from the beginning he had other women. Still, I didn't like sharing. Jerome would dress me like a princess wearing five-hundred-dollar raw silk suits and the best in whatever I needed. He would always take my outfits off the top. Then Kenny would buy the shoes to match all my outfits, and we would dine together at some of the more finer places in Detroit and Canada. On one of my birthdays, Kenny took me to Canada to see Sammy Davis Jr. It was awesome. Sammy sang happy birthday to me at our table. It was one of the best times ever. I was in a soft yellow raw silk dress with sequins and pearls. I was looking lovely, and Kenny loved having me on his side. He was a gentleman that was proud to have this beautiful, sharply dressed brown sister on his arm.

As time progressed, the neighborhood was getting worse and so was my drinking. I told myself it was time to go. I let Kenny know I wanted to move and I needed a down payment for the house I was getting. He gave me a couple thousand in cash. That was the first time my kids had seen so many hundred-dollar bills. I just came in the door and threw it in the air. That was a delightful moment mixed in the middle of the raw hurt that I was trying to free myself from. Not only was I drinking, but I was also smoking marijuana like it was normal. I've had three homes, and I have grown marijuana plants in all of them. I was very proud of my beautiful six-feet tall plants. When times were rough, I sold marijuana to cover my bills. I had the best around. I wanted to believe it would help me not to drink so much. I was using cocaine and sniffing it, too, but it wasn't so much my drug of choice. It was never as strong as drinking and smoking weed, which for me, was just a natural thing to do.

As far as I was concerned, it was natural for some people, and for some others, habit or addiction. I decided there was a difference between wanting it daily and having a daily need for it. I didn't want to accept that I had a habit and a desire to feed that habit. It was easy to call what I was doing the natural thing to do. I thought that way for many years. Today, I believe it was an addiction, but during those years, I named it what I needed it to be. It was like taking a valium. However, making my mind up to stop was rough. Yes, I wanted to smoke when things got bad, but most of the time, I managed. As far as sniffing cocaine, I did it socially and when I wanted to escape. I'd get into a hard-hitting blues song like one of B.B. King's which would make one feel so bad, like a ball game on a rainy day. In retrospect, I can't see any sense in the craziness of it all.

After a while, I had to stop listening to blues or any songs that would make me feel like I was sinking down into depression. Some music can be healing, or it can have one become stuck on stupid. Songs like "I Can't Stand the Rain," if it keeps lingering long enough, a person could be soaked in the rain and feeling helpless. I thank God my escapes were periodic. I was able to come out of them with a couple of days rest and a few hot baths. I was trying hard to soak the alcohol and other impurities out of my system. I knew the danger of it sitting in my body if I did too much of it. It was always my intention to help myself, and it was a method to my madness.

Jerome hooked me up with a realtor who found a beautiful, three level red-brick home. It had vines growing all over it, with a white rod iron screen door, and a lot of windows. It was the prettiest house on the block and it was now ours.

We moved in and my children loved their new home and their schools. Meeting our new neighbors was very different from what we knew in our past neighborhoods. It was a different experience living in a diverse community. The people in that community lived well and cared for their neighbors. Life was going great, although I was still dealing with my sisters moving in and out disrupting our way of life to accommodate them. It was easier just to make it work and help them so that they could get on their feet sooner. Sadly, they just never took care of business.

My friends would ask me, "Why do you keep doing this to yourself?" My reply was, "somebody had to do it," I felt responsible. I had been doing it all my life. I always talked to God and asked Him, please help me with your children, they are yours, and I don't want to be old and beat up after the job is finished. I always asked Him to renew my strength like the eagle. I asked Him to give me compassion to love my family but all I seemed to get were heartaches that affected me and my children.

It was always drama, after a while, that depressed feeling came to me strongly. I was still trying to deal with guilt, condemning myself, and feeling sorry for myself. I began to isolate myself and drink more. Finally, I eased out of Kenny's life. I didn't want to hurt him. I told him I just needed time to get myself together. He was sad, but he gave me space. Jerome wasn't happy that I was drinking so much. He didn't drink and didn't want to see me drinking. He didn't come around that much, but when he did, it was like the first time we met. We always had a strong love for each other, but I just couldn't seem to get it together. I was losing it and isolating myself from my real friends.

My best friend, Earnestine, thought I had moved to California when I left my first house. We had such a beautiful relationship, and we were like sisters. We both had three children. When she needed to get away, I kept the children, and she did the same for me. There were also times when we managed to go out together. One night we were out together, and she met the love of her life through a mutual friend of ours. He went back to my house with us, but she ended up leaving and left him there with me. I called her and asked why she left without him. Somehow, she believed he was interested in me. But I corrected that, said to Earnestine that he was hitting on her, and I was sending him to her, so I could go to bed. She was alright with that, and they have been together ever since, happily married over forty years now. She and I had a special bond. I felt terrible when I moved without telling her. I didn't want her to know how bad I had gotten. We have now reunited. Earnestine's daughter, Sandy, found me on Facebook and connected us. I needed to rekindle our relationship and God made it possible.

Chapter Eleven

NEW FRIENDS, NEW TROUBLE

I met some new friends, and they were some roughnecks. I wasn't in their league at all, and I thought I was too much of a lady to be playing with the type of fire they brought. But on the other hand, the alcohol and my low self-esteem led me to believe I wanted to be bad to the bone, too. I began to hang with one guy from the new circle of friends, and it was downhill from there. I didn't have the get up and go anymore. I stayed out of the bars because I drank too much. I didn't have the money I was used to having. When I had it, I didn't know how to handle it, and that was something else to add to my sorry party. Trying to recapture those times in the past is still hard for me.

Hooking up with Lamar weighed me down. He didn't have any income, so I was trying to get away from him, and it was hard. One day I told him we had to end our thing. The mortgage was due, and he couldn't help me, so I needed him to get out of my way. He, on the other hand, was telling me we could find a way to get some money. I asked how and what we needed to do. He said the only thing I had to do was drive and of course, I said, "Ok let's do it." We went out and robbed seven places, service stations, bars, and liquor stores. We were the black version of "Bonnie and Clyde" for a hot day. It was wild and one of the craziest things I have ever been a part of. I was never afraid, and I didn't think anything through before doing it. That was the way I was since starting to steal at a young age. Again, it was just a natural thing to for me to do.

We got the money that was needed and more. It was as simple as that. Lamar went in to get the money, and I drove the getaway car. Just thinking about it makes me break out in a cold sweat. This action was another layer of guilt and condemnation. The last place we did, was way out on the 8-mile road in Detroit. While I was waiting in the car for him, I heard glass breaking, and then gunshots ringing out. My mind said, "time to go." I merged in traffic, and all I could see in the rearview was a black guy running toward the car yelling, "Stop the damn car." I slowed down enough for his butt to climb in the window, but I never stopped moving. He was mad, he looked up and said, "You were leaving a brother." I told him, "As scared as I was, I would leave my mama."

After performing those "Bonnie and Clyde" feats with him, I felt I was stuck with him. It was hurtful that I was a part of something so sinful, and the fact that I didn't give doing it a second thought, showed me the person I had become. I didn't like it at all. I didn't want anything else to do with him. Having to deal with him gave me more shame and guilt. He was sleeping in my basement. In my heart I just wanted that spirit to be gone out of my house, and out of my life. He was bad medicine. When a person abuses the gift and image God created them to be, it welcomes destruction. He chose me to be His child, and I always knew that, but I still went through some crazy times. The weight of so many things on my shoulders, I allowed it to cheat and rob me of what and who God called me to be. I thank God, my Father that He will never leave me or forsake me. Even though I have sinned and played the fool, I'm reminded of (1 Samuel 26:21 NKJV). Then Saul said, "I have sinned, return my son David, For I will harm you no more, because my life was precious in your eyes this day. Indeed, I have played the fool and erred exceedingly."

I still saw Jerome months in between, and one night he came by. I was grateful Lamar hadn't been around in a few days. We had been talking about our situation, and how unhappy I was with him in my life, and in my home. When Jerome dropped by, it was always good times for both of us. It was refreshing just thinking about, how it used to be. I wanted things to be the way they used to be between us when I cared for him. I had cried so many nights in my alcohol and weed over the years about not having him all to myself as I wanted so badly.

I conditioned my heart to know it could never be. I enjoyed Jerome, but I knew after many years of me not being the one and only, it would end. It would be one less thing to hurt over. Our night was beautiful and magical, like a fairy tale. Knowing I would wake up the next morning, in his caressing arms, then gone again until our next time together. There wasn't the next time. That was our last time together. When I'm done, I'm done. During that last night, neither one of us knew it would be our last one. He pulled me close after making passionate love to me and holding me tight. He would always do that, as if knowing one day, I would no longer be in his life. We had a sincere love and respect for each other. I just couldn't handle it. He knew I would eventually cut my feelings, and he would not be able to penetrate through them. He would need a special key to open those feelings again, and he and I knew he wasn't ready to give up his lifestyle.

The next morning as we laid there asleep, I was awakened by a cold and frightening feeling. God has always shown me when danger is near. I sat up, and Lamar was standing over us with a knife in his hand. Jerome didn't wake up. I eased out of bed and proceeded to lead him to the basement. I was pleading with him to please not hurt Jerome. I never wanted the two of them to meet. I never wanted Jerome to see that I had slipped that low. I asked him to please stay down in the basement until I could get Jerome up, and out of the house. He agreed. Lamar said I wanted to get rid of him in order to bring my old love back. He implied that his motive was to hurt Jerome. I knew I would have to say some serious prayers to my Father to help get this unwanted spirit out of my life. I had to get my act together and fast. I knew that kind of behavior could never happen again.

Meanwhile, I had to get Jerome out of the house. When I went back upstairs, Jerome was washing his face and brushing his teeth. When he saw me, he pulled me close and asked what was wrong. He said, "You look like you just seen a ghost." I was thinking, *if you don't get out of here, you will be one.* He lingered for a few minutes getting dressed for the golf course. I finally walked him downstairs while feeling very nervous. My demeanor concerned him, so he told me to lay back down for a while. Then he was gone, maybe for a long time, so I thought.

I went back to the basement to talk to Lamar. Once Jerome was out the door, I no longer felt nervous, just mad as hell. I told him that I have had a relationship with Jerome for many years and that we would always be lovers and friends and that I have the final say. I told him that no one dictates what happens in my life except me. It didn't matter that I believed that it was over between Jerome and me. He needed to know that period. I wasn't at all scared to put him on notice. *"Who do you really think I am?"* I thought as I was talking to him. I may have fallen into the dumps, and have you in my basement, but I know how to fix this thing.

From that moment on, I knew I had to pray him out of my life. I got serious asking God to please help me. I prayed to God, "I'm not happy, and I have a heavy load on my back, I don't have my peace and joy, and I want it back." I was nowhere near as strong in the word as I am now, but I knew that my God is bigger than my past, pain, anger, and fear. My pastor, Linda Hodge, says, "Prayer is a legal transaction that is recognized by God." She is so right.

I knew by calling on Him and asking for His mercy and grace; He would remove Lamar out of my life, and that is what happened. Lamar had several warrants, and he was picked up and sentenced to jail time. I don't know how long of a sentence he received because I never went to any courts hearings. I was happy that he was out of my life. Because I wouldn't take his calls, so he would write letters, and one day I received a letter from an inmate saying Lamar was killed in jail. I wasn't happy the man was dead, but I was pleased, that I would never have to see that dark spirit again. Praise the Lord.

With that load off my shoulders, I knew it was time to make plans to leave Detroit. I had to go, that season of my life was over. I had my eyes on California, I had been out there once and could see myself there. When I was seeing Kenny, he purchased a first-class plane ticket for me with champagne and the red-carpet treatment. It was cool being it was my very first time flying. From that first time, I fell in love with flying. I am too scared to ride a Ferris wheel and I can't drive with tall mountains and steep hills all around me, but put me on a plane, and I love it.

Kenny and I had a friend in California and, my Marie was there. I also wanted to find my oldest sister, Florene. I didn't know at the time that she had passed away. When Mom passed, I located her through KJLH radio station. She didn't call me, but her doctor called and said she was having open heart surgery and it wasn't hopeful. He said she had a fifty-percent chance of pulling through. After that, I didn't hear anything. I didn't know whether she made it or not. I didn't have a follow-up number to reach out to her. That was something else to hurt for, not knowing what was happening with her.

Many years later, I found her father and went to Memphis to see him after learning my sister hadn't made it. I was hurting and crying buckets of tears because I didn't get a chance to see her again. Hearing that my sister died alone, wondering why her sisters weren't in the picture. It felt like a knife cutting through my heart. I told the family I found and read a letter Florene had written to Mom. She asked why she didn't tell her that she and I had the same father. I didn't know Mom was even keeping in touch with her or knew her whereabouts. Florene died by herself and without her sisters being there for her. How freaking awful is that? I was talking to Mom in my head. *I asked her, "why she didn't want her children to have contact with one another. Are you scared they're going to blast your butt"* You *are so very wrong Mom. That was not cool at all.* It took me years to forgive Mom. I think it will be many more to forget.

I confronted her father, Ike, and asked, "Are you my father?" He denied it. His wife broke out and started crying, she grabbed me and held me. I looked just like him because he was a little short brown man. His wife, Ray, probably felt at that moment that Mom and Ike were still slipping around. She probably had doubts before, but looking at me, she knew. She was hugging me and crying, as for him, he dropped his head and continued to deny it.

I knew in my heart he was my daddy. I am at the realization that until this very moment, I have never thanked God for being able to say I met and confronted my daddy. He must have told Florene, and she confronted Mom. Mom hid the letter under her mattress, and I didn't find it until after she died. Ike must have needed to get it off his chest and tell someone. He wanted my sister to know so we could bond more. Perhaps confronting him in front of his wife made him feel he had to deny me. Maybe he thought he had to protect his marriage of many years. My mind was racing as I thought about the hell he must have been in. He knew Mom well. She had left her firstborn, at the age of five years old with him.

I would have loved to have known my sister's whereabouts. The thought of her dying alone without knowing that we didn't know where she was, hurts to the core. Again, so many hurts. Many people don't have the opportunity for closure, so I say with tears that I am very grateful that I did. Thank you, my Father, for closure. I remembered when we were kids and Ike coming to see us. He was a barber who loved playing the piano. I remembered how he would love on me more than my other sisters. He would kiss me and hold me close to him. I didn't like his wet lips on me, and until this day, I can still feel him kissing me. I guess he loved me in his silent way. I used to ask myself, "Why is he kissing me?"

When his wife looked at me, she could never control her tears. She held me close to her heart and gave me so much love. I gave my daddy chances to own me, but he continued to deny me and took it to his grave. But that's ok because I have a heavenly Father. I am so grateful that God stayed on me to write my story. I would never have put it together and been able to say I met the man that fathered me. Even if he couldn't admit it to me, in fear of hurting the woman he was married to for all those years, I am truly grateful. I know now a little bit more than I knew before.

I would never allow my mind to think on the things of my past because they hurt too bad. Many times, I tried to stop writing, and God would tell me, that it wasn't all about me. I understood that I had to continue to write. I was still caring shame when I started writing. I thought it was my idea to tell my story. Since God was involved, he was the one letting me know it wasn't all about me. He knew this book would be a blessing to many because He had allowed it to happen. Knowing if God can save a wretch like me, He will do it for others. In the end, He will get the glory.

Once again, I had plans for a new life. As I began to plan, I prayed. I was saving money by not paying any bills, not saying that was a wise endorsement, but at that time, I did was I knew to do. Now, it was just the four of us, my children and me. I had a meeting with them to see how they felt about moving to California. I tried to involve them in making changes. I was so young dealing with so much drama. It felt like we were all raising each other. I've always believed, when I can see the vision I can make it happen. My children understood that we were about to leave our beautiful home and friends. My children seemed to understand I had to move fast and that I was fighting for my life.

It was now or never. I had to get out of the rut I was in because it was not the way I wanted to live. I had to get away from sisters and family. They were like gravity, pulling me down. My son's birthday was coming up on the 27th of December. We agreed the only money that was going to be spent for Christmas would be just for dinner. I asked my son if he wanted birthday presents or California. He chose California. We made up our minds to move in January 1974, and we were acting on faith. We started packing right away. I got information from Greyhound, and I could board three boxes per ticket. A month before we were ready to leave, I picked up the boxes and started to break the house down. We packed up enough for a two-bedroom apartment. I had everything for the kitchen and bedrooms. I had lamps, all the beddings, and bathroom items. I had twelve large well-packed boxes, and each one of us had a carry-on. Phaedra had her dolls, Bridgitte had many books. Joe, he stuck close to me. He was my protector from day one.

We were leaving that old depressed life and entering a new one. My children and I were so happy for this new adventure. I was praying more than ever. Before I talked it over with my children, I spent time with God telling Him all about it. I had peace and was ready to go.

A young single mother, in her late twenties, making a giant move like that, with three children was significant. We weren't moving across town but states. I didn't have a roadmap on raising children. I just knew how to care for them and be a provider for their many needs. Not having anyone I could talk to about my problems, I was always functioning on my own. I got it right sometimes and blew it many other times. When my kids got pissed at me for screwing up, I would tell them to tell God about it because I did the best that I could under the circumstances, so blame it on my head and not my heart.

When it was time to go, we were happy and excited. We left at night, on the nine o'clock Greyhound bus. After getting everything taken care of, a friend came down to see us off. I had a few drinks, and by the time we got settled, and the bus pulled out, it all hit me. The drinks and pressure of leaving knocked me out.

I thank God, for making it happened, and I gave Detroit one last look, and said, "I thank you, and see you." Detroit was good to me even in the hardest of times. I never blame my downward spiral on the city. I knew

God was moving me to a better place. I knew my mistakes were my stepping stones to my success. I had the same exciting feeling that I had after I gave birth to my Phaedra. I was ready for California. It was going to be good for my kids and me. So, I laid on my son's lap and felt his arms protecting me, and I slept.

Chapter Twelve

GOD IN THE MIX

We woke up in Chicago, and a young lady got on the bus with three small children, an older son and a younger set of twins. We started to talk, and she asked me if I wanted a drink. She pulled out a fifth of a Canadian whiskey blend. I'd never drunk that before, but we drank all night as the kids slept. By the next morning, we pulled into the rest stop for our first meal. My kids and I were hungry, and we were anxious to get off the bus to eat and drink. We noticed that the young lady and her kids weren't moving. I went back to the bus and told her, "Let's go, our children are hungry." That's when she told me that she had no money. I stepped off the bus and went to my kids to tell them and asked what we should do. Bridgitte said, "Mom, you know we will have to feed the children, so get them off the bus, and let's eat." Bridgitte was always like me in many areas, and always second in command. I valued her opinion. She was my child, my best friend, and support when I needed her. I told the young lady, "come on, let's eat," and the kids beat me off the bus.

I had to pray to God not to let my little money run out because I had four more mouths to feed. We had a day and a half, and a night left to travel. Every time we ate, they ate, three meals a day. God is awesome. I know now, God used me to be the angel for them. He knew I wouldn't let them down. She was going to Oceanside to her husband, who was in the service and he was not aware she was coming. I felt sorry for them both. Alcohol makes you do some crazy things. I'd been there, even though my kids didn't experience not eating for days. I drank, but I also took care of business.

We rode out of the snow and into the sunshine. It was as if I could see God smiling in the clouds as the sun shined. I felt so close to my Father on that ride. I felt His presence all the way. Everything was going well as my kids were happy and glowing. Bridgitte and Phaedra had their dolls and books, and Joe was full of excitement. We talked about all the things we were going to do. It was the best move I could have ever made.

We arrived in Los Angeles, happy and ready to start our new life. The young lady stayed on the bus headed to Oceanside. I gave her money, so she would be able to contact her husband. We hugged and said goodbye. God knew I would take care of his children and those he had placed in my care.

Marie and her boyfriend met us at the station, and we went to their apartment after eating dinner. We were tired and wanted to lay down, so Marie gave us covers and blankets to make pallets on the floor. We were happy, and I knew I would have my apartment in the next few days. I didn't waste any time as I was out looking early the next day and found one in South Los Angeles. The manager said we could move in after a day or two, but I asked him to please make it a day. That night, we went down, exhausted, but we knew the transition would be over soon.

The next morning Marie had a blackeye. I thought I saw something strange with her boyfriend the first time I laid eyes on him. I tried not to focus on it, but when I saw the blackeye, I knew what I saw and what I felt about him was real. The guy was abusive and crazy as hell. They were taking pills commonly known as "black beauties and red devils." The black beauties were uppers, and the reds devils were downers. I knew for sure I had to move fast.

While the apartment was being prepared for our move in, I went to a used furniture store. I bought twins beds plus living and dining room furniture for next-day delivery. On the third day, I picked up keys to the apartment and went to get my twelve huge boxes from the bus station. I told Marie's boyfriend that he needed to rent a trailer. He argued that his big truck would be enough. I gave up trying to convince him, and we headed to the station. When the baggage attendants showed her boyfriend my boxes, he was shocked and so was the bus managers. They couldn't believe one person had the bus company to haul all those boxes across states. Wasn't long after that the bus company changed their rules to one box per ticket. I shut that three boxes per ticket down. Even as I write this, I am laughing out loud.

We went to get a trailer to load all the boxes, and by the time we got to our new place, they were delivering my furniture. That night, our new home was complete, and we did it in three days. Look at God! My Father, awesome in every way. The apartment was already clean, but in any place, one should clean the bathroom yourself. We cleaned our bedrooms and bathroom and prepared to rest. Knowing we were in our home and didn't have to go back to my sister and her crazy man, we could sleep and rest that night. We had everything we needed for the moment and we were happy again. We gave thanks to God. The goodness of the Lord, His mercy, and favor made it such a smooth transition.

The next morning, we had our breakfast in our kitchen, with our skillets, pots, and pans. I heard what sounded like rocks hitting my window. I looked out, saw a man, opened the window, and he told me his name was George. He said he saw us when we were moving in. His line was that he lived in the building and couldn't wait to meet me. He told me that he was seeing a woman downstairs. However, he wanted to see what I was all about, and offered to assist me, should I need to go out for groceries or run errands. He gave me his pager number and said we could meet around the corner. My natural instincts kicked in and I recall seeing him in a station wagon and I knew I would have it at my disposal. I could use someone to help me navigate the city. I knew it was wrong to use this man, but I needed his help, and so I used him. We started hanging, then six months later, I used his Veteran's G.I. housing assistance to buy me a house in Inglewood, which was a step up from where the kids and I started. I was in my new home within nine months.

During our stay in our first home in Inglewood, I met Al, who picked up where George had left off. George's time was running out. I started feeling guilty because his lady was pregnant, and the baby was coming soon. I told George that our season was over. I mentioned that we could always be friends, but he needed to go back to his beautiful baby he created while we were hanging. I told him after we moved he could start being the man he's supposed to be with his girlfriend and child. I even suggested he get married and buy her a house. I also told him whatever happens when I sell the property that I would be fair to him.

I felt terrible for a minute, but I wasn't as strong in the Lord at that time as I am now. I knew who I was, however, I was still straddling the fence. I had left my dream home in Detroit, and nine months later, I had two houses, one in the front and one in the back. It was a blessing. God has always been good to me. We stayed in the house a year before the bank bought all the properties on the block. My thoughts were that the bank could offer more to buy my house. All the neighbors were selling out right away, but I kept holding out for more money. The banker told me bulldozers would be tearing down my home, and I should take their offer. Each time they said that, I would make them offer more. My house was the last one standing, and I accepted the best offer. I was led to believe that I received the most out of all the neighbors that had lived there for years.

After George and I stopped hanging, I let him know that whatever happens when I sell the house, I would be fair to him. After the bank paid me, I was upright with George, and he was able to get his family a better place and had money for extras. It was a blessing in the end for everyone.

While we were still living in Inglewood, Joe had the back house, and we were having serious problems with him disrespecting women. He felt he had his own house and didn't have any responsibilities in the front home. After trying everything I knew to make it right, I called his father and asked him if he would take him during his senior year. He agreed and that's when I got the ticket, picked him up from school, and headed to the airport. He put up a fight, but when my mind is made up, it's made up. We closed that chapter.

I moved to Van Nuys, in the San Fernando Valley, after selling our first home. Oh, happy days! I was able to get a beautiful, three-bedroom apartment. It was spacious and airy with sunshine streaming in. I had plenty of money from the sale of the house. I fell in love with the Valley the first time I saw it from the top of the 405 freeway. I have a phobia about hills and being too high up, so I knew from day one, it would be a challenge for me, but I still wanted to be a Valley girl. Each time I drove down that hill, I prayed to God for strength. I would always remind Him, that He did not give me a spirit of fear, but of love, power, and a sound mind, but I would also tell Him I knew all that, but I was a little scared with sweating hands. It took some time, but I finally got over that one with the help of my Father. I was panicking one night as I was creeping down the hill. I asked Him to please help me get down that hill. He said look back and as I did many cars were coming at a fast speed. I said, thank you, my Father, and put the foot to the medal, and proceeded to outrun the traffic. From then on, I was ok with the 405. I said it was a piece of cake.

Now back to me and Al. Our relationship was not a match-made in Heaven, but it was what I needed at the time. Or so I thought. When I met him, we were drinking and snorting cocaine on weekends. One night I drank too much, passed out, woke up, and Al was shooting cocaine. Without much thought, I asked him to give me some. He fussed a while, but I'm sure he was tired of waiting until I passed out before he could shoot up. He may have been relieved that he didn't have to hide it anymore. It became our thing to do late nights on the weekend. When we were thought to be sleep, we would be shooting up. It went on for about a year, and toward the end, I could see a little puffy vein on my arm. I was getting scared that my kids were going to find out. I knew I had to leave it alone.

I was thinking how it would break my kid's heart if they caught me shooting up. I prayed, and by the grace of God, He made a way out for me. Al was mixed up in some things that the FBI was investigating, things he had me and some of my friends involved in. He had a friend that was creating fraudulent income tax returns and needed addresses to send the checks. We allowed him to use our addresses. However, the FBI was onto his scheme, and it didn't take long for them to start tracing the checks. I tore up the one that came to me a few days after receiving it. I got scared and freaked out as I remembered my prior history with cashing checks I wasn't supposed to. We were all interviewed by the FBI and said that no one cashed checks. The FBI came after Al after they played their fear card on us for a while. He was arrested and taken to jail and received two years while I received probation for my involvement.

It was now time for me to quit using the stuff. I thanked God that I had recognized my problem and had prayed hard about it. I asked God for a way out. I cried out so many other times before, He heard me and removed the thorn. I experienced what it was to detox; it wasn't good at all. My body craved for it a few times, but I prayed the desire away from me. I held onto my favorite scripture; "Greater is He that's in me than he that's in the world." I was able to stay clean and get away from it.

Bridgitte got pregnant, with her first child, Donald. She almost had the baby before I knew she was pregnant. I was still drinking from time to time, but not like I did in Detroit. I was still depressed and using marijuana since I was growing six feet tall plants on the side of my house.

Bridgitte started to put on weight, and being a big girl already, to me it seemed like she was putting on more pounds. I never in my wildest dreams, would have thought, she would be having a baby. Like mama like daughter. She had this beautiful baby boy. He brought so much joy to our lives. She was fifteen, making me a grandmother around thirty-something. Now I had to step up my game. I was going to be a grandmother. Bridgitte would have to go back to school, not like her mother. I was determined, that she would have that baby, and hurry up and get back in school. We put a plan in motion.

I met with her principal and teacher, and they tried to give me a hard time with her coming back, but I told them, she was in good health, and I would bring her and pick her up. She got their approval. I picked up her school work, so she could work at home until it was time for her to return. She went back as a teacher's aide. Bridgitte was a smart girl. All my children made good grades and were gifted.

I stopped drinking when Donald was born. I had to make sure that Bridgitte made it to school. Donald went everywhere with me even to drop off and pick up Bridgitte from school. When he started talking, that's when it got rough because he would talk from sunup to sundown. When Donald went to Headstart, I started making him read everything. He was reading at home and learning at school. I would make him read billboards and street signs. He was able to read a business letter from beginning to end. Donald was pronouncing words that kids don't learn until third of fourth grade. At five years old, he was an exceptionally, smart kid and we were extremely proud of our little guy, who loved to dress and wear cowboy hats with all his outfits.

With Donald in school and Bridgitte going to school and working at the VA hospital, I felt it was time for me to start taking classes to be able to work in an office. I was through with the bars plus I wanted a job with real benefits. I enrolled in Jobs for Progress, a government-funded program, and received office skills training. After a few weeks in school, I became friends with Jerome, and later he became more like a brother to me. We learned we were from the same neighborhood in Detroit. We lived on Turner and Jerome, and his family lived on Tuller Street. He admitted they used to chase my son home. Small world. We became great friends, with our families coming together, such a joy. I had a brother to look out for me in California. We were in school for a year then I got a job with the AAA (Automobile Club of Southern California) as a switchboard operator.

After two years, I was promoted to cashier. I loved working with people, meeting them, and making new friends. One of whom is still considered a best friend today is Cynthia. When she came into the club, she asked, "Where are all the black folks? I said, "on the third floor in emergency road service. I am the only black, on the first floor." We had another black guy in insurance and sales on the second floor. But there weren't many black people around. Cynthia and I became best friends. She and her husband, Melvin, were trying to get pregnant. They had been married for eight years, and now wanted children after enjoying their life and traveling. They tried for a long time and weren't able to conceive. I told them, "it's time to pray." We got in agreement and started to pray. As a result, and with help from a fertility program, Cynthia finally got pregnant with her first child. I asked to be the godmother of her first son, Rashaun. I felt like I had helped to play a role in asking God to please let her get pregnant. I experienced the same connection for many years, with the next two children, Cherina and Julius. I didn't have to ask, they just claimed me as their godmother, and I love them dearly. They called me, God Willie. They all have made me a great godmother to their children. I love all of them. They are my family.

As I continued to work at AAA, I decided that I wanted to be a medical assistant. So, I resigned from AAA and went to Western Medical College. It was a new and exciting time for me. I was able to study and get excellent grades. I wasn't sure if all the smoking and drugs had damaged my brains. Studying at home was a challenge. I would go to the park and study because my house was full of my up-and-coming family and their friends. It was easier for me at the park or locked in my bathroom in the tub for a couple of hours with a big water bottle with ice. After three months, we moved into the clinical lab. Oh, my word, what did I get myself into? There were arms bleeding and students excited about drawing blood, and I was sick to my stomach. I wanted the medical side not the clinical. Again, that was how I had always been. I jumped into things, without really seeing the whole picture. I just knew I wanted to help people and saw myself as a medical receptionist.

There I was again, in another uncomfortable situation, that I wasn't happy with. I didn't want to draw blood, and hell to the no, you can't draw any of mine. I knew that was ending real fast. I had to get out of that place. I didn't want school anymore, and so that ended the job. But God gave me favor. I didn't have to pay any of the student loans. After a few months, I went to a temporary job agency and applied for a job.

Chapter Thirteen

ADDICTION

My first assignment was with a large aerospace company. I'd seen the building before. It was a beautiful glass building about a block long. When I saw it for the first time, I said to God, "Father I would love to work in there." I didn't even know what they did. I just wanted to be working there. I landed a job in the phone room, so I was in the door. After a few months, I was called into Human Resources. They offered full-time status to me. Look at God. When I started, I fought with the head of Human Resources. She wasn't nice to me. I felt she was looking down on me, and after haggling about the money, I felt the "need" to tell her what I thought of her and the company. She wouldn't pay me what I was worth, so we argued. It was just over three months since I had left AAA and I wanted the pay I was making there. She finally said, "Willie, you will be on probation for ninety days." I said, "and so will the company." I agreed and signed papers for my new position, excused myself, and went back to my job. From then on, I fought for every opportunity I could for more money. Every job review was all about the money.

My next assignment was a switchboard operator in that beautiful building. I remembered when I first asked God to be in there. *Ask and you shall have, knock and, the doors will be opened.* One never knows how it's coming but having faith that it's coming makes the difference. This new and exciting time in my life made me happy. I was glad to be off my 90-day probation and started receiving my benefits again. My hope was that I would soon be back making the salary I was making with my former employer. I was, with a little persuasion, begging, human resources and letting them know I needed to make more money. That was the way my twenty-seven years went with the all three of the major aerospace companies.

Phaedra was always making comments about my need for money even when I had a nice little nest egg. I would be talking about having more money. She always told me, if I stopped shopping, I would have money. I couldn't quit because I loved it too much. It took a lot of money to raise my children and provide for them in a manner that I dreamed. Many responsibilities came with, raising my sisters and their children. At a young age, I had to care for a village. I was always trying to see where I could get that next dollar.

My first meeting with black brothers at the company started with Stan. He was talking with a few brothers, and I asked, "where are all the black folks around here?" They said, "You're are looking at them, with the exceptions of a few more." The company had been ordered to hire more minorities. I liked Stan and he was very supportive in my times of need. He also made sure I met the right people for fun and job promotions.

We became best friends, and we still are today. I had gained another brother. He looked over my immaturities in the huge aerospace industry. Stan took me by the hand and helped me get my act together. He looked out for me and introduced me to the few people that weren't in my area. I decided to go back to school and took word processing classes at night. I got in the door, but it was not my intentions to stay in the phone room. I had become too comfortable there. I was still smoking pot and drinking, not a lot but too much. I was thankful for my job, though it wasn't stimulating. I could hang out and party all night and still do my job and take a nap on the couch in the phone room on my break and lunch hour.

Six months later, I was introduced to crack cocaine by a couple of male friends one of which was a brother. I was always adopting brothers. I had four sisters, and I long for a brother since childhood. I never planned to do crack cocaine, but it just happened to be in the place I was visiting. I said yes, what the heck. The first time I tried it, I liked it. I had never experienced it before. It was something that made me want to dip a little bit more, so I played with it for a while. But things spiraled to where I spent way too much money one night. I spent rent and bill money and by the time I realized what happened, it was too late. After smoking for a couple of months, I cleaned my act up fast and stayed away from it. I was determined to leave it alone. There were danger signs, I even thought about allowing myself to play again. So, with the strength that I could only get from God, I started crying out to God. I always prayed for strength to walk away from danger, knowing it could get the best of me.

One night, Pearl came over with the pipe and a few nuggets. It was enough to get me started again. I had never done this with her. The devil had to be in the mix for her to show up and dangle it in my face. It was something we didn't do. We didn't get high together. She didn't smoke weed and wasn't a big drinker, so we didn't hang out together. I always took care of family business especially when it came to her and her children. My mind was to keep it moving. Still, we had nothing in common. It was a set up straight from the pit of hell and it got me in a bad way.

There we were in my bedroom, hanging out, getting high, when in walked Phaedra. We were busted. I didn't even hear her come in. The look on her face was one I had hoped to have never seen. She looked shocked, mad, disappointed, and disgusted. She was seeing me for the first time getting high and I didn't know how to handle it. Although, Phaedra was grown, working, and doing her thing, I was always more afraid of my children finding out about me more so than becoming addicted. I believe God used my daughter to bust me, knowing that I would quit after that. The devil set out to hurt me, but God used it to bless me.

I never feared getting hooked. I always knew when it came to heavy drugs, that I could walk away. I had done it before. I was using alcohol as a crutch. As for marijuana, I just loved smoking it. I didn't have to deal with crazy stuff when I chilled out and smoked. I guess you could say both were a crutch. I would go to AA, Alcohol Anonymous, and had a wonderful time, vowing to stop drinking. I spoke at many speaking engagements. Leaving AA, I would always light a joint, and drive off thinking it was a good meeting. Marijuana was a way of life for me. I didn't see it as something wrong or habit forming. I viewed it as a way to calm down. I would rather smoke marijuana than a cigarette, and when it came time to give one up, the cigarettes were the first to go.

That was the last time I smoked crack cocaine. I came face to face with my worst nightmare. It was the best thing that could have happened. Who knows, I may have continued down that road as so many others did. I thank God for never leaving me.

I was sobering up and grateful to be closing that chapter of my life. I was still going to school at night for word processing. One day, Stan told me about an opening in Configuration Management. I interviewed for the position and got it at the same time. I finished school and received my certificate in word processing. However, I never used it. I didn't consider it waste because it did introduce me to things I wasn't familiar with and helped me in other areas.

I got the position and I felt good about myself. God gave me another chance and much favor. I loved my new supervisor and most of the people were pleasant. One of my co-workers was Fran and we hit it off right away. I had two other close friends that I met during my time in the phone room, Janice and Sandra. We formed a strong bond. We didn't know it, but God knew it, and was strategically weaving the pattern. Later, Edie came into the picture. She was the department's new secretary. We all had love, and respect for each other, and always spoke of the Lord. Letting the world know, we were believers in Christ. I fell down many times, but God always lifted me back up. I was stronger and better than before and more determined to do His will. My Pastor, Dr. Fred L. Hodge says, "As Christians, we can either win or learn, never do we lose."

I lived in guilt, condemnation, and shame for so long that I would slip from time to time, even with being in God's word. To clarify slip, I mean I would hit a joint when I would be out of town or around someone who was smoking, and I would always feel guilty about it. Whatever I did wrong, I would feel guilty about it. It was as if I had to have something to deal with, major or minor.

God would have mercy on me, embrace me, and lead me back in His word. So, with those new friends, we decided to start a Bible study group during our lunch hour. We would meet and pray on the grounds, or sometimes, we would go to Janice's house. We gained strength and knowledge from praying and encouraging one another. We would pray for everything. When it was my turn, I would get so emotional with tears, and seriously cry out to the Lord. I knew God was cleansing me in a real serious way. No one had any idea of the life I led just months before our studies. He who began a work in us will be faithful to complete it. We knew it was God bringing us together, and keeping us together, even until this day. We are grounded in His love and glad for His tender care.

Pearl continued smoking and went all the way down. I threatened to drop a dime on her if she didn't get off the pipe and take care of her children. But she was too far gone. My son did it for me, not telling me anything until the next morning. Joe had walked in and didn't like the situation. Pearl had a bunch of guys in the house hitting the pipe. Her daughters were in the bedroom scared to come out. He called the police, and they took Pearl, and the children away. Pearl went to jail, and the children went to the court. I found out all this the next morning. I had to go to court and decided to take care of the children because Pearl was going to be incarcerated for a while. Bridgitte went to court with me and encouraged me to take the children. She agreed to help me with them.

I didn't have a problem taking the children home. The younger one, PJ, was my heart. She was seven at the time and the oldest, Nicole was thirteen and a problem. She didn't like me, and the feeling was mutual. I was hesitant to take her, I felt that she would act a fool, and I would have to light her up. I was right; it happened three months after they came with me. It was horrible for them to have their mother locked up in jail. PJ and I, we were cool, but Nicole was just ugly, despite me trying to be there for her. She was disrespectful and just nasty. As I said, I gave Nicole her three months, understanding that being separated from her mama was a lot for her, but she was too much for me. I tried to give her time before lighting her up, after that, I was forced to do it. She caught me on one of my worst days.

My car battery died, and I was working to get another one. In the process, a check came up in the system that had not cleared, and that prevented me from getting the battery. I didn't have AAA card at the time and no cellphone. During all that, I had some blocks to walk to Bridgitte's house to pick up the girls. As I walked in the door, very happy to be off my feet and an opportunity to sit and map out my next step, Nicole rolled her eyes at me for something I said. It was on. I told her, "Let me speak to you in the bedroom." We were walking down the hallway when she realized what was going down. She turned to me to go the other way. I said, "too late…you got to take this beat down, I am ready to light you up." And I did. She never got stuck on stupid with me again, and she had much respect for me. I love my family, but I will light them up, and I will win by any means necessary. I can't lose. That was always in the back of my head.

Pearl, who is bigger and crazier than me, tried to fight me. I had to fight her from the third floor to the basement. She was determined to win, but I knew if she won, I would never be able to live that down. She would use that to manipulate and disrespect me. I started praying, knowing I was running out of air and I was tired. I asked God for strength to win by any means necessary. I was able to get a choke hold on her and demanded her to stop, or I would break her neck. She gave up and never said a cross word to me again. She would go off on everybody, but not me. I don't play with kids or young adults being disrespectful.

The day after lighting Nicole up, I went looking for a car. I was led to look at new cars although my credit was poor. I couldn't buy a battery, but there I was looking at new cars. I selected a brand new, stylish and beautiful black on black car. I was at peace filling out the paperwork while the salesman was happily making a sale. However, something changed when he left the room to check out my credit. He came back in an unprofessional manner. The salesman told me I had poor credit, and no one was going to sell me a car. I said thank you and left the building. I was sad but not hurt. I was at peace not knowing how I was going to handle all I was going through because I had faith in God to handle it. The next morning, I called my friend Shirley at our company's credit union and told her what happen. She told me to bring the paperwork to her, so she would see if she could help.

Two days later she called and told me to come pick up a check for over ten thousand dollars or whatever the car amount was. Shirley said to me that I didn't qualify for the loan, but God told her she had to help me. By financing the car, she was putting her job on the line. Shirley said, "when man says no, God says yes, and she had to listen to God." I picked up the check and went back to the car lot and told the salesperson to get my car. It blew his mind, and I got the opportunity to share a little about the God I serve. I shared with him that God never leaves or forsakes me. He considered what I shared with him about the Lord.

The girls were with me until they graduated. I thought Pearl would take her children with her when she got out of jail. When she got out she said, "better you than me. You got them, you keep them." It sounded like something Mom would say. She said, "you can take care of them better than me." I thought, *what the hay*, she made one of the most important decisions in her life. There I was again, raising children. As bad as I wanted to say no, I saw the progress the children were making, and I had to continue to help them. God always made a way for us. For the first six months, I had no help with them financially, but they were well dressed and had everything they needed. We worked hard with them, they were doing their homework and just being little girls. It all paid off because they came out of special need classes and fared well. They needed to be taught many things. However, Phaedra was a blessing in helping me with them. Sometimes it was overwhelming, working and caring for them and sometimes, I just didn't feel like homework and whatnot. My children were smart in school but working with children that didn't advance as fast was new for me, but we persevered, and God gave us much favor.

Chapter Fourteen

DRUG AFTERMATH

I was able to get off the crack pipe, but Bridgitte and Joe had issues. They just couldn't seem to shake it. Some people can take one hit and be hooked for life. My two went a few years. Joe was hanging tough, so tough that he owed the drug dealer a large sum of money. Word on the street was the drug dealer had threatened to kill Joe if he didn't get his money. I said, "The devil is a liar, in the name of Jesus." I found out where the drug dealer lived and knocked on his door. One of his henchmen opened the door and invited me in. I told the henchman I wanted to see the one that had a hit on my son. The boss explained who he was and that it took a lot of nerve for me to come to his drug house. I told him I would do whatever I had to do for my children. There were guns, drugs, and ugly faces all over the place, but I wasn't afraid.

My mind instantly went back to my Detroit days, and how I ended up in a notable drug lord's house. Oversized black garbage bags were full of money, and those guys had machine guns all around. I was there with one of the top lieutenants that I was dating at the time. He said he had to run by for a moment, and he wanted his boss to meet me. I remember praying to God as soon as I entered the house, my mind was saying, *danger, danger.* I immediately started praying, asking God to please send his angels to watch over me until I left the place. I promised I would never go back again, and I didn't. Now, there I was many years later, in another drug house. Small time thugs compared to the ones I knew, but they were lethal and very dangerous. I gave them much respect. I spoke like a woman with confidence, power, even though I didn't have all that. I had God on my side and they were no match for the mighty angels that went in with me. So, I wasn't alone or afraid.

I told the drug dealer if he gave me a couple of weeks, I would have all his money. I let him know that my word was all I could give him at the time. He agreed, thank God. I knew God was my protection before I entered the drug house. My angels covered me in the den of thugs and drug dealers.

I am glad they gave me a chance and wouldn't harm my son. I shook his hand, and we had a deal. He gave me a strange look when I returned a couple of weeks later with all the money. He counted the money and confirmed it was all there. I had paid the debt in full. I shook his hand again and thanked him. Perhaps the strange look was because he had never seen anyone make good on their word before. I left it at that and went out the door. My son was saved and was finished smoking after that. Joe knew by the mercy of God, he was saved by His grace, and that would sustain him.

Now Bridgitte hung the longest. She was strong in so many ways, but with this thing, she was weak, and it took a while for her to get herself together. Through it all, I always had faith that she would pull through. She had my blood in her. I'm a fighter. We go down, but we must get back up again with God's mercy and grace. Bridgitte went into a downward spiral from the time she was introduced to the crack cocaine pipe. It started off slowly, then progressed as money permitted. She was also having problems with Henry, the children's father, Eboni, and Tonie. By the time Bridgitte and Henry realized what had hit them, they were both in bad shape. Bridgitte decided to move to San Diego to get away from him because she wanted to start a new life. I was instrumental with helping her and it cost us a lot of time and money helping her with that new start.

I learned that things had gotten out of hand with Bridgitte when I received a call from Tonie. The first part of my intervention was getting the children to pray for Bridgitte to get some help. She continued the downward spiral a year and a half after I had gotten the call from Tonie. One night I was jolted out of a deep sleep by God. I asked Him, "what is this?" He said, "it's time to pray." Immediately I rolled out of bed and on to my knees and started to pray asking God to take care of my child. Somehow, I felt it was an urgent alert to cover her. I felt she was in trouble. I had to stand in the gap for my daughter's life.

Later that week I was speaking to her on the phone. It was not a superficial conversation. I was digging deep, probing her with opened ended questions which meant she couldn't give me just yes and no responses. I was trying to discover what was happening with her. She told me that she had to call the paramedics because she was passing out periodically. She told me that the grim reaper was taunting her and telling her he was waiting for her. As she explained it to me, she painted a picture of how he started in on her. She said she could hear his voice in her head. She told me she opened the blinds in the house and she could see him.

I could imagine that she was being attacked in her mind and her body as well, though I didn't understand what the attack was to her body at the time. When the paramedics revived her after what she described as passing out, they told her she had almost left this world. From that point, she sought professional help through a drug and alcohol recovery system. It was a long road through the recovery process, but she knew she was close to death. She wanted to live then more than ever. She knew she had a fight and she believed she was strong enough to endure. She also knew she had a support system with her family and counselors that was praying for her recovery as well as her life. Thank you, Father, for waking me and sending angels to help my child in time of trouble. Standing on (Isaiah 54:17 NKJV). I prayed no weapon formed against me and my family shall prosper.

My covenant with Jesus is to take care of my children and my children's children. I would remind Him of that sometimes. I am serving and believing in You. I would say, "I trust that you will save my children and bring them back sane." This is my heritage for serving our awesome and amazing God. However, it caught up with her and things got very bad. I told her I was coming for my babies. Toni, 11, Eboni was 9. Her oldest, Donald, was 15 at the time. He came with me for a minute but went back to try and take care of his mama. It just seemed the generational curse was getting the upper hand.

In retrospect of my Mom, she has cirrhosis of the liver at age forty-seven. She must have been hanging, too. Back then, they drank the liquor called "white lighting." It was strong rotgut stuff. She seemed to have liked it. Sometimes we ate beans every day, but Mom managed to have a pint of white lighting under her pillow from time to time. She was always sweet talking some guy into buying her some or a forty ounce of beer.

I was always close to my grandchildren, and when things weren't going right, I could always count on Tonie to find some way to tell me. She would get pissed and let it be known, saying, "I'm gonna tell my grandma," and she did. She knew I would take care of business by any means necessary. She knew I was coming to bring them home. I made the phone call to Bridgitte and said, "I am on my way." She didn't hesitate, and Bridgitte didn't fight with me. She knew when I said I was coming, I was already on my way. She knew the kids would be better off with me until she could get herself together. Phaedra and I got ready to care for two more children. The plan was put in motion for the trip to San Diego to get the children.

It all happened shortly after the 1994 earthquake in the San Fernando Valley. All I could think of was I have to get the kids and get a larger place. I was still shaking from the quake and aftershocks, thinking how scary it was and how I lost it. Phaedra and I reversed roles. She was the mother, and I was the daughter. The quake hit hard around 4:30 am. I had just made my run to the bathroom and back to bed thanking God as I always do. A few minutes later, I was knocked out of the bed and woke up on the floor. The shaking of building was violent. I couldn't stand up without being knocked down. I was crawling on the floor. I would try to get close enough to put my hand on the doorknob but just couldn't reach it. I shouted out to God saying, "Please Father in the name of Jesus, I've got to get out of here." Suddenly, I was lifted to the door where I could feel the knob. When I said lifted, that is just how it happened. The angels were there to lift me to the door. There is power in the name of Jesus.

As I opened the door, Phaedra was coming for me, I grabbed her legs and started to cry and say, "I want to move to Atlanta, want to move away?" I don't want to live in California anymore. Phaedra was calm and said, "we can't go right now because we have to move fast and get out of here." I was so proud of her in her new role because I just lost it. I was a mess. After we got out of the house, she went to different people to see if she could help. It was pitch black outside, but we saw a rubber tire company was on fire around the corner. The only thing that could be seen was the smoke, and the smell of the tires burning was horrible. It was like being in a dreadful movie. From time to time, I could feel the ground shaking from the aftershocks. This was so overwhelming to me, I was in tears because I didn't have my toothbrush. Funny now, but not then.

We moved from a two bedroom to a three-bedroom house, and for two years we had bunk beds on each side of the room. It was a little cramped, but everyone was happy. Phaedra and I took care of our babies with no help from my Bridgitte. We told her we just wanted her to get herself together and Phaedra and I could handle the finances. God always provides. Sometimes Phaedra had good jobs, and sometimes she didn't. During that time, the movie industry was slow, and many folks were out of work. We lived off credit cards. Sometimes we didn't have money, but no one missed a meal.

After a couple of years, Bridgitte finally cleaned herself up, with the help of God, prayers, and counseling. She got off the crack pipe and prepared to receive her children back. Happy days were here again. They were going home, and I was on my way to bankruptcy court. I was pleased they were going to be reunited with their Mom, and my daughter was looking healthy, and ready for a new start, plus some of the pressure was off me.

During their stay with me, I had three different schools in the morning to drop kids off, and they would catch the bus home. By the time I got to work, I had to catch up, have coffee, and pray nobody put me to work with hot packages right away. It was hard, but we made it work. We had many challenging times, my oldest niece, Nicole, was always trying to take her anger and hurt out on PJ, the youngest one. PJ never played with dolls, but there was one she loved and wanted. The doll's name was PJ Sparkles, her namesake. Nicole broke the head off and threw the doll out the window. Nicole didn't like the relationship PJ and I had. We hit it off the first time I saw her in Detroit, in a rat and roach infested building. The same conditions I endured as a child and when I was all grown up. My heart went out to that then 5-year old child with the saddest eyes. I think I reached out to her because I had those same sad eyes. The only picture I have of me as a child. I knew I had to get them out of Detroit.

I ran away from my family seeking a new life without them. Pearl was okay living that way with two young girls. I went to visit them to see how things were and then, I had to do something about it. I came back home and put them on the prayer list at church and prayed to God for help to deliver them out. My kids were young adults, and I was a grandmother. I believed I could help without neglecting my children. I put a plan together to bring them to California. I had a friend in Detroit. One of my exes, who kept in touch with me. I called and asked him to pick them up and get them to the bus station for me. After explaining the problem, he did. I sent him money for their bus fare and food. I felt he would take care of them for me. I told my sister to pack up their clothes, leave everything else and to please try not to "bring" any critters with them.

We had a beautiful three-bedroom house with a large patio covered with grape vines. We also had a pretty yard with a lemon tree. We loved our dream home. It was hell bringing them into our world, after being away from them so long. It didn't take long to see my sister hadn't changed. I had to hurry and put a plan together to get that chick out of my house.

After a couple of months, she was moving in her place. I didn't like it for myself, but it was like heaven to her compared to what they left in Detroit. She was back to her old ways, jumping from place to place. I was always running trying to help her. After a few years and the crack pipe, everything came to a crashing end. She had to spend time in jail and rehab, and the girls were coming home with me.

When they came to live with me, PJ was happy because she and I were always together. Every time she could hang with me, she was rushing to ride in the car with me. Nicole didn't care for this, so she did as much as she could to make her sister's life miserable. After she destroyed the doll, the only doll PJ ever wanted, PJ felt like it was on. They were fighting for the first time when Tonie screamed, "Grandmaaaaa." I made it in their room just in time to see PJ throw a hard punch to her tummy. It knocked all the air out of Nicole. She doubled over as she grabbed her stomach. I must admit that was a happy day for me. I'd been telling PJ to stop letting her bully her and to stand up to her. After that Nicole never bullied her again.

Now Ms. Eboni, my youngest granddaughter, was a little sneaky. My first fifty-dollar bottle of Fashion Fair foundation came up missing the next week after I purchased it. The smooth caramel color was perfect for my complexion. The Fashion Fair sales rep had tried many colors before getting the right one. I was so happy to have it. Early one morning, I was looking for it, asking everyone whether they had seen it. As we rushed to be out of the house at our regular time, I was getting desperate, so I kept asking if anyone had seen it. Rule number one is no one touches my makeup, or any of my personal things. That was something I had to get to the bottom of and make sure it never happens again. I was going to be late for work, but I didn't care. I told them they may be late for school, as I said, "This doesn't happen, and somebody is going to tell me something."

I looked under my bathroom sink, and there was a face towel looking like the color of my makeup. I knew right away that Eboni did it and I gave her a chance to come clean. She lied to the bitter end. Eboni realized I wasn't giving up, and finally confessed, and said, "I just put a little on my doll's face, and I liked the way it looked so I put it all over my doll." She was always into make-up and hair styling, even as a small child. I lost it, I took my shoes off and started jamming on her. She was running all over my bedroom. We were the same size, and I worked on that butt until I was out of breath, and she was screaming as if I was killing her.

That was my first time I tapped that butt. First, you don't lie to me. Second don't ever mess with Grandma's things. I didn't care if the neighbors could hear and thought someone was hurting her. That's what I was trying to do. We lost a lot of time getting out of the house. I had to move fast, but I was tired after all that butt kicking. I thought, *What a life!*

Bridgitte's recovery was going well, and she was getting herself together to get her children back home. She was excited about her sobriety, and we were forever grateful to God for strengthening her to kick the habit. She got her apartment, and we helped furnished it. We rented a truck and took the children's beds there. We loaded our living room and dining room furniture, too. It was our way of helping her, plus get new furniture for our home. It worked out; it was a new start for all of us. Eboni was happy to stay. Tonie wasn't thrilled. I think she loved the valley and being with us, or she just wasn't sure how things were going to work out.

Nicole was almost ready to graduate and would turn eighteen. She had plans and so did I. After graduating, Nicole started staying out late and disrespecting me again, letting me know she was grown and no longer had to follow my rules. I told her that was absolutely correct. Nicole said she would leave if she couldn't do what she wanted. I told her to let me help you pack. In twenty minutes, I had that chick packed and ready to leave my house. She was shocked and couldn't believe what was happening. I loaded her suitcase up, and we headed to her mama, Pearl. We surprised her. I said, "I am bringing your daughter home." She was surprised, and I told her, "better you than me, see ya, wouldn't want to be ya." A big burden lifted off my shoulders. I was so glad to unload that chick because she was getting ready to work my nerves, and it wasn't happening. I was prepared to be free from headaches, from children, or so I thought. I had always asked God many times to please don't let me be old looking, after raising His children. I asked Him to please renew my youth like the eagle.

I was ready for a relationship. I'd been celibate for ten years after my last fling, and 12 years before that. I was trying to walk right. I stumbled sometimes. I called it a fling because it was a desperate and lonely move that I made just for one time, and I regretted it for many years. After being tied down with kids for so long, I desperately wanted a real relationship. I met this beautiful giant of a man, named William, or so I thought. We weren't spiritually connected. I thought maybe if I take him to church and show him the way to the Lord, we could work on being a couple or something. We did go to church together, but this brother had something else on his mind. He would always say how much he admired me as a born-again virgin. I liked him a lot, and one thing we had in common was he, too, was an alcohol and drug counselor.

I graduated with my counseling certificate after two years in college. We were very passionate about helping folks stop drinking and using. After hanging for a while, we started sleeping together. As I was on my way to hook up for an evening out, Phaedra's best friend Tracy, made a statement. She said, "Willie don't go out there and be fast, don't do it, Willie." Somehow, she felt that I was getting ready to go way out there and do something I would regret later. I wish I had listened because it was the worst sexual mistake I could have ever made. I had gotten much closer in my spiritual walk, but my flesh became weak. I knew I was about to sin long before it happened. There was a force so strong drawing me into it, and I knew I would be committing fornication, and yet I continued. I wanted it that much.

Single women and men are properties of the Lord and we are supposed to keep ourselves until we are married. I had fallen twice in twenty-five years. One day God woke me up, and I felt like Eve in the garden naked. Even though I had my pajamas on, I couldn't feel them. I rolled out of bed to the floor and started to weep, and asked God to please forgive me. God always allowed me to step out of line, but He always comes for me. The shame that I felt during that time, and long afterward made me end the relationship. When I told William that I couldn't continue, he laughed and said, "I knew if you were as strong in the Lord as you said, you couldn't continue anyway." I said to myself, *Satan in the flesh, danger, danger, get far away from this man as fast as you can.* God is so awesome. He moved the man, not only out of my life but out of the state. He said he had a vision that his mother was ill, and he needed to go home to New York.

After several months, he called and told me God told him I was to be his wife. I responded to him God had not told me, so keep it moving. That was my last time, I was still waiting on God to allow my husband to find me. It was okay though because I knew, it was all in God's time. The man was gone, but I was left with Hepatitis C. I was in denial for a long time, thinking that the Hep C came from my drug use. When I got honest with myself, I knew I had contracted it from William. Let your guards down, and the devil will be there to take you out. Lessons learned, there are consequences because of sin.

Everyone was out of the house except PJ, and she became a handful. She totally lost her mind. She was skipping school, acting selfishly, and rebellious. Phaedra was trying to tell me she was out of control. I was giving her enough room to hang herself. When I saw her report card and all the days she had missed, I went to her school. I was going to do some damage control. I was so mad, but someone tipped her off that I was on the grounds. That chick was not to be found. She knew I wasn't going to be nice. I went to get her, and I didn't care who was around. She decided it was better to be home to talk with me. She was the sweetest kid until maybe fourteen and that's when I noticed her changing. I always tried to protect her, but one can only do so much. When she turned eighteen, she didn't want to abide by my rules. She moved out, and I was okay with that. I am finally free with no children.

My son was married and had a beautiful daughter. Her name is Tia. The marriage lasted for maybe a year. His wife left and left Tia, too. I believe my son was a lot like his father, abusive, or feeling like she should be at his beck and call. He was controlling. She made the same decision that I made except I took my children. I guess she had to decide who the best parent would be for her child. She also knew we would be there. So, the women in the family banded together to help Joe with his daughter. Bridgitte played a significant role in helping. She took care of Tia, while Joe worked. They lived in the San Diego area, so I could bring her home for the holidays and take her back.

Happy days didn't last long. Mae, my younger sister, was diagnosed with lung cancer and died in three months. She was special to all our hearts. Mae touched each of us in her own way. I was feeling off for a while like something just wasn't right. God has always put it on my heart, and in my spirit when something is getting ready to happen. I knew the Holy Spirit was leading me to get things in order. I knew because I felt the urgency in my spirit to do it.

I had to hurry and get to Mae the last weekend of her life on the earth. One of my dear friends was getting married in Vegas, and I knew I had to be there. But as soon as we made it to the reception, we said our goodbyes. We headed back to the Valley. Sandra and I had rented a car and on our way back, I was driving and it dawned on me that I had left my glasses for night driving in my car. It was dark leaving Vegas and Sandra was no help because she didn't drive at night. She offered me her glasses in a laughing way. We had a good laugh about that.

Normally my vision would be blurry, but God opened my eyes, and it was like I was driving in the day. It's always a blessing seeing God step in and carrying me. Urgency was in my heart. I knew I had to hurry, get home, get Shamika (PJ), get rest for the night, and head to San Diego early the next morning, to go see about Mae.

It was the same feeling I had when my retinol detached as I was heading home in a rainstorm. I knew something was wrong but couldn't figure out what it was. I couldn't see out of my left eye and as I struggle to see. I told God, "My windshield wiper on the left is not working, but if I lean over I could see." Not knowing how serious it was, I just talked it over with God and told Him I would ride through the storm with Jesus. I was so calm knowing Jesus was in control of me and my car. Big water waves hit the car and I was tossed around pretty good. My little Rav4 was no match for the heavy rain, and I was making my mind up to get a Jeep after that. I was thinking to buy a heavier vehicle and not be caught driving a small car again if I could help it.

I made it home that night and I got up and went to work the next morning. By the end of the day, I must have seen a thousand little spots, and as I tried to read something. I was about blind in my left eye. I knew then this is something serious. I went home, changed my clothes, got in warm sweats and got water. I didn't know what was going on, but I knew it would be a long night and whatever it was, God would take care of it. I headed out to the hospital where I was told surgery would be right away. Praise my Lord and Savior, I only lost forty percent of sight in my left eye after surgery, and my doctor said glasses would take care and I would be just fine.

Chapter Fifteen

PREPARING FOR THE UNKNOWN

When I walked through Mae's door early that Sunday morning, the first thing I said was, "We need to pray." She had such a beautiful glow on her face. It was hard to tell she was as sick as she was. We prayed, and after loving on each other, we went to visit Pearl. We had lunch and enjoyed our time together. Mae went to the hospital that following Tuesday. She called me on Wednesday and said, "Sister, I know you may think I'm not saved, but don't worry I am. I have been going from room to room ministering the gospel to the sick people." She also said, "I am ok, I know the Lord." *Look at God.* He knew it would hurt me badly if she weren't saved. The next day Mae was gone. My baby was gone. The hurt was back again. My sisters were like my children. I raised them from babies, and they looked to me as a mother figure. They didn't have that mama's love, even though she was there with them. She didn't know how to give love. My sisters would let everyone know, that their mama didn't raise them, they would say, "my sister raised me."

We lost Marie's baby daughter, Little Fran. I was big Fran. Marie's oldest daughter, Eunice had left the family long ago. She was addicted to heroin. My lasting memories of Eunice was seeing her scratching her body in need of a fix. I picked her up and brought her to the valley with us, trying to see how I could help her. Eunice didn't have any of that in mind, for her, there was only heroin, and it was taking her over. I couldn't help her, I took her back over the hill, and that was the last time I saw her. She was another one of my family members that I lost. I accuse generational curses; they were the culprits of my losses.

Little Fran had a daughter named Andrea whom we loved to care for. From the first two weeks until she was five years old, Bridgitte and I took care of her. Bridgitte's son, Donald, and Andrea played well together and got along. Little Fran enjoyed her freedom, and we believed we could take better care of Andrea and so we did. She was happy for a short time. In spite of having a rough life, I'm not sure if Little Fran was ever content. Andrea broke the family curse of having babies and not taking care of them. She became a mother of eight by the age of thirty-eight and was the best of best mothers. All her children strived to be the best. They were "A" students all the way through school. She didn't play and always demanded the best from her children in behavior, goals, and accomplishments. Andrea wouldn't accept anything less and didn't let her crazy childhood and lifestyle dictate who she was. Andrea believed in not only her children getting an education but she was always taking classes and finding ways to improve her life.

We had a small family as it was, so when they started to pass away, it was an incredibly challenging blow. After Mae passed, Pearl passed a few years later from breast cancer. It took a while to get that happy feeling again. I held on by thinking I had to thank God every day for waking me up and starting me on my way. It's up to everyone to decide what we do with each day.

Pearl had been sick for a long time. Cancer is no joke. It was a real concern for me to learn that Pearl was not saved when she got ill. No one wants their family member not to know the Lord. It's what you know that will keep you, living or dying. I had a group of Christian sisters, and we called ourselves the "Posse". We prayed together and worked in the counseling department at Faithful Central Missionary Baptist Church in Inglewood. When I told them about Pearl they said, "We must get to San Diego, and lead her to the Lord." These women were some deep sisters and knew the power of prayer. They loved the Lord and didn't mind kicking the devil's butt. I was so touched that they would take the time and do this for me and my family.

God placed in my life, the most powerful women of wisdom and love. Three of them went to San Diego with me, Jeri, Sandra, and Judith. Pat and Chanae stayed behind to pray and intercede for us. We had a great time talking about the Lord, making sure Pearl understood what giving your life to Christ means and was sincere in giving her life to the Lord. Hours later, we were at war in prayer against the devil who didn't want to let her go. Satan showed up and tried to hold his ground with loud noises of every kind. His presence was like a giant black crow hovering over us, but we didn't care. The louder he got, the more we prayed. We were pleading the blood of Jesus and we weren't backing down from the devil.

Pearl was always entertaining unfamiliar spirits, and when she would try to tell me about it, I would say to her that I didn't want to hear it. While we were praying for her, I finally understood what she was trying to say to me. I saw for myself how the devil was interruptive and combative in her life. Sandra was praying then suddenly, she stopped. She told us later that she couldn't open her mouth, and felt the giant crow hovering over us. When I realized that Sandra had stopped praying, at that moment, I felt something was around my throat choking me. I started to pray and called him out and said, "I know who you are. You have no authority over this house, prayer group, or my sister." I pleaded the blood of Jesus and told him he must leave in the name of Jesus. That force was so intense. After that, Sandra was able to resume praying. That's when I knew I had something powerful inside of me.

The thing I had run away from all my life, I was now able to confront. Before that day, I had been in earnest prayer, after my friends told me Pearl didn't have long to live, because of what Pearl said. I shared that with my friends. They said that satan did not want to let her go, and prepared for a battle. I was new to all of this. I knew of satan, but I never encountered openly fighting a war for a soul.

I knew the women with me were tremendous prayer warriors, however, God wanted me to know I had gained power through praying and using my faith. Pearl was led to the Lord and transformed from the hellraiser she used to be. Pearl was happy, peaceful, and with a big smile on her face. She didn't live long after her encounter with Christ, but I am so pleased she was saved. I know where her spirit is, and I know she will never suffer again. As Christians we believe, "to be absent from this life is to be present with the Lord." This belief will save a person from so much grief when you lose a loved one. I know she's home and I am ok. I am still grateful for the prayer warriors who walked with me through the journey of saving my sister. "I will love these prayer warriors always, for the love they showed me, my sister, and family. Again, I say, friends, fill that void where family avoids."

After my two sisters passed, Phaedra and I went on the Inspiration Mediterranean Cruise to Greece hosted by our former church, Faithful Central Baptist Church. We traveled with Bishop Ulmer and his wife. After all, we had been through, the timing was perfect. We both needed the getaway and we were ready. I didn't have a hundred dollars in my purse when it was time to leave. After paying bills, tithes, and offerings, I didn't have anything left. I didn't care because I had American Express and would transfer that money to my account. The American Express representative said it should be there by the time we land in New York and when we got off the plane, the money was in my account. I was making jewelry and took a few pieces with me and was selling it on the route to New York. I had made close to four hundred dollars by the time we landed. I learn that when I do what I am supposed to do, God takes care of the rest.

It was a blessing from the time we got on the plane and as we flew to Venice to board the Holland America Ship. The menu had Phaedra's middle name on the top—Alitalia. We knew from that then on it was going to be a great trip. And to think Phaedra, never liked her middle name We found out we weren't pronouncing it correctly, but after discovering the correct pronunciation, she loves it. We flew to Venice, Italy to board the ship which was about a six-hour flight. When we arrived, we rushed off the ship and boarded a high-powered motorboat. The driver asked if anyone wanted to drive. Phaedra quickly took the wheel and was flying up and down the Grand Canals. We have that same view on a picture in our living room, and who would have ever thought we would be there. I always wanted to see it, but, the picture on the wall was as far as my dream took me at the time. But I serve a good God, and He gives me the desires of my heart.

Some of my most memorable places were Dubrovnik, Croatia, Santorini, and Rhodes, where we visited Phaedra's Hotel. It was a transforming time for Phaedra. She stretched out her arms and said I am home since her name originated from Greece. She felt good. On that day, Phaedra and I decided to take a Mercedes Benz cab around Rhodes and loved it. We'd heard about the hotel and just wanted to do this on our own. We didn't want the tour with our friends. The experience was personal.

Then we were off to Ephesus and Turkey, walking down the white marble roads, which were over two thousand years old and still beautiful. During our time there, Ephesus was being restored. It was one of the greatest ruined cities in the world. Many archaeologists were working and digging all over the grounds. The Celsus Library had a tunnel that lead to the Ephesus brothel and the Scholastica baths. It is still hard to believe they had a system that heats the water in those giant pools. The baths were heated with the hot air that passed through below the floor called a hypocaust. Amazing for that time.

After that was the Church of Virgin Mary. It was an education center for training the Ephesian priests. It is the first church built in the name of Virgin Mary. These were very spiritual moments. We visited the marketplace and many other exciting places. We were walking in the footsteps of John the Baptist, and it was a mind-blowing and an incredible experience. Our last stop was Athens, where we visited the Parthenon a former temple, on the Athenian Acropolis, Greece, dedicated to to the goddess Athena. That was one of the great highlights of our trip. We were grateful we had a chance to see this beautiful and spiritual time in history and to know that our Lord and Savior was a part of it.

Before our Greece cruise, we moved from one aerospace company to another. The company was under the same umbrella but, a different name. We were meeting and dealing with new management and supervisors. It was a rude awakening for me. It seemed like a third world country. I knew God placed me there to make a difference in my co-worker's lives, but it was strange. It seemed as if were constantly under a microscope. We had to ask to use the phone to make doctor's appointments, and they were strict regarding being on time. I was not used to any of this. Edie, myself, and Janice were the director's pets at our former company. There, we could do just about anything we wanted if we did our work. The new management company was heavy-handed, and micromanagers and I wasn't going for it. The supervisor callously talked to the girls, with no respect. She made the mistake of doing it to me one time. She embarrassed me to no end in front of a customer at my window. Thank God I was remained peaceful.

In Bible study, we were studying 1st and 2nd Peter. I was learning how to have a quiet spirit. I would go to the bathroom and talk to God. After work, I went to Bible study and then home. My spirit remained at peace. I called my manager and told her what happened. I informed her, if her supervisor ever did that to me again, I would speak to her, in the same manner, she spoke to me. I went on to tell her if things got out of hand with her, I would take her to HR. Thinking how many managers I bumped heads with, I am good at giving a voice to a situation. I respect others, but I deserve that same respect.

The next morning, my supervisor was called into the manager's office, and later she came out and apologized to me several times. She had a new respect for this little brown girl. My co-workers, on the other hand, took any and everything the supervisor dished out. I knew it would take lots of prayers to get this thing in order. The girls believed in God but were having significant issues, maybe that's why they didn't complain about our supervisor.

Sonia was having a hard time talking about her son. He was killed in a car accident when he was sixteen. Sonia couldn't understand why God let it happen. I was careful speaking to her about God because she didn't want anything to do with God. I had a plaque with the 23rd Psalm on it that my dear friend, Cynthia, had given to me. I asked Sonia if I could place it on her desk. I told her that maybe when she was ready to speak about God, she could then give it back and we could take it from there. It took her a minute, but she came around and was very peaceful and happy.

My other dear friends, Susan and Sandra, were having problems praying sometimes. Praying with a group was difficult for them. Susan was in a horrible marriage, and that evil spirit that was causing problems in their marriage was on her every time she tried to pray. I was familiar with that devil. It was time to pray and kick the devil's butt. I was so ready to start putting a plan together to deliver Susan. I was beginning to understand what my assignment was. As much as I tried to feel sorry for myself being in this situation, God would always speak to me and comfort me when I would cry out in the bathroom.

We received another sister into the group, Kathy, who was a Mormon, and she prayed well. I respected her, and her willingness to volunteer when I asked if anyone wanted to open in prayer during prayer and Bible study time. It all started when God put it on my heart to ask them if I could take them home at lunch and pray with them. I was five minutes away. Little by little, I had them praying. They were making progress. It was beautiful seeing their growth in the Lord. Allowing them to want and understand true worship and do it in such a delightful way.

Then the Lord put it on my heart to start a Bible study. By that time, Sandra had transferred from to our former company which now made it six of us. We began reserving a conference room for our prayer and

Bible study. It was glorious. Not only for the Bible study, but for the bond of love and respect for one another we were forming. We kept growing and teaching each other.

Many months later, Edie was transferred to our Woodland Hills location. I was so happy my dear friend had come. She was also my walking buddy. We walked together for many years, on our break and lunch daily. I was elated. She joined our group making it seven for Bible study once a week. It was awesome. We were all growing in the Lord and learning scriptures. I wasn't judging myself about my past because I didn't live there anymore, however, I was still dealing with unresolved issues. I had anger issues and a habit of holding on to stuff. When you work in an environment that was as toxic as that one was, one couldn't help but get angry or hurt. Sometimes I would get mad or upset and handle it well, and other times, not so well. The group was helping me, as much as I was helping them.

Our supervisor continued to do ugly things to remind us that she was in charge. She had said something to me one time that hurt me dearly, and I headed to the bathroom to talk it over with God. He said, "It's not personal." Praise the Lord for being an on-time God. He would let me know that our spirits were clashing. The supervisor was Hindu. After that conversation with God, I was able to handle things better. God told me to continue to pray, and not to lose my peace. Eventually, our prayers worked, and the supervisor was out of the department, and later out of the company. She had been there for over thirty years. Look at God. I felt I was sent to bring them to a closer relationship with the Lord, and to do some house cleaning. We did that, as well as learned many valuable lessons from each other. Our group gained strength knowing who we were in the Lord. Their conversations changed, and they had begun to experience the love of our Lord and Savior.

We are still dear friends today. They held me up during the passing of my sisters, niece, and my daughter. These ladies were my strength in many ways as I was for them, carrying them in their times of loss and hurt. We were super strong as friends, and I love them dearly. There were three of us in the department who lost children and then the director's son died while he was parachuting. As we loved each other, we were able to embrace him and believe me, he ran to us for support, knowing we all had been through it. God strategically placed us together to help ease our pain. God knew when he said; "I know that hurt, we would be a blessing to each other. Being confident of this very thing, He who has begun a good work in you will complete it until the day of Jesus Christ" (Philippians 1:6 NKJV). Thank you, Father, for the many powerful sisters you have blessed me to be a part of my life.

I called these sisters my silver sisters. My other sisters, Fran, Janice, and Edie are the golden girls. I have always desired sisters to love me as I did them, but my biological sisters never could give me the love I needed, so God made sure I had sisters that love me for me. I have tried to give my friends the love I so needed, and they have showered me with tender love and care. Not just these powerful groups of women, but so many others across the country. I am truly blessed. I am the King's kid, make no mistakes about it.

What blows my mind to this very day, with all the ugliness that I've done and the shameful life I have lived, He knew me from day one in my mother's womb, and He loved me still. Through my weakness and my faults, He chose me as His child. I am grateful and thankful that He never left me or forsake me. I thank Him for His mercy, grace, and so much favor. I love you, Father God.

Chapter Sixteen

SAVING BRIDGITTE

My covenant with Jesus is to take care of my children and my children's children. I often reminded Him that I am serving and believing in You. I would say, "I trust that You will save my children and bring them back sane." It is my heritage for serving our awesome and amazing God.

Bridgitte had a few happy years after her bout with crack cocaine, but she just couldn't keep it together for long. The attack on her body was diabetes, high blood pressure, and being overweight. The health issues were the results of the abuse she put her body and the wear and tear from not taking care of herself. She was not in good shape at all. Phaedra and I decided to bring Bridgitte home with us, so we could help her get well. It was the best thing that we could have ever done. We had so much fun having Bridgitte with us during that time. We revisited some of the lost years and brought life to the ones we could enjoy. We went shopping and screamed for the Lakers while watching the games. We loudly rooted for Barack Obama as he was zeroing in on becoming the first black President of the United States of America. It was joyful to hang out with one another. It had been a long time.

There were so many fun things to do. I believed celebrating and enjoying life together was good medicine for us all. Bridgitte was keeping her doctor appointments and Phaedra and I were going to work. When we came home, there would be nonstop talking between us until late in the evening.

I purchased a couple of photo albums and she spent the next few weeks putting all the twenty years of photos I collected in order and placing the images. It must have been an inspiring time for her as well. Many people don't have a chance to look back over their lives, but God took her back down memory lane. I think it was two of the happiest weeks of her life to be able to recall all those wonderful years. Our family had many happy times, as well as sad ones. How great Thou art. She came to live with us in October that led to a great Thanksgiving together and soon Christmas. It was pure joy and happiness with all the family. The three of us went Christmas shopping for presents, food, and just had fun together. I knew Bridgitte had medical problems but, I was praying she was going to get proper care and she would be okay.

On one of her doctor appointments for a full physical, the doctor told me her heart was good, and the things she needed to work on. He also said, if she took better care of herself she would be fine. I tried to accept that but, I would make my bathroom run at night and see her sitting up sleeping. Deep inside that always bothered me. I prayed, "Lord, please take care of my child." I ached for her for many years, not just when she came home with me, but years before.

We also found out Bridgitte had sleep apnea about a few weeks before she passed. Sleep apnea is a potentially serious sleep disorder in which breathing repeatedly stops and starts. She needed a continuous positive airway pressure machine to open the airway, so there is no collapse in the throat while trying to breathe. We were waiting on approval from her medical insurance for the sleep apnea machine. I am sure she needed the machine years before being diagnosed.

Christmas of 2007 was our best yet. All the girls were home and the men were in San Diego, on the phone talking with us all the time. We all were together and happy. We had a house full, my niece and her friends were over, and I remembered how exquisite the food was. The Lakers were winning, not to mention Barack Obama was winning the presidential race. We were all together for the first time in a long time. We said a beautiful prayer before opening gifts which is something we always did. Giving thanks and honoring God for the abundance of love, family, and all our blessings. Our Christmas dinner was the highlight of our day. Everyone helped with the preparations. We were all eating and talking with our mouths full, excited and happy. After our meal, everyone was hanging out around the house while I was in the kitchen washing dishes and cleaning as usual. Everyone pitched in and helped to put the house back together, but I added my special touch. Suddenly the Lord spoke to me and told me not to lose my peace and joy. He said He was ready to drop some powerful words into my spirit. That's just the way God speaks to me. I stepped back, looked up, and said to Him, "What up with this? I don't understand." He repeated it saying, "Do not lose your peace and joy." I didn't understand it. It hit me hard. I just started praying, not sure what I said. I just knew it was time to pray. "In the name of Jesus," was all I remember saying when I finished.

We watched the Laker's game, and Bridgitte was screaming, just as loud as we were. Everyone had a good time. Later that night, I put myself to bed. I left all my girls up as they continued to have a great time. They hadn't been this happy in years. Earlier that day, I prayed and asked God for a special blessing for each of them, calling each out by name. It was all God, and it was a powerful prayer. I remembered Bridgitte saying, "Mom, that was a wonderful prayer for each of us." It was like she was hearing me pray for the first time. It touched her heart. God wanted her to know just how He loved her and how much love she received from family and friends. The prayer did what God intended for it to do. Reaffirming the love that a mother holds for her children.

I kissed them all goodnight, one by one, and Bridgitte said, "Mom, I love you" and I told her, "I loved you too, baby." Those were the last words that I heard from my daughter's mouth. The next morning, she was dead.

It was the morning after Christmas. We thought she was sleeping hard. My granddaughters and I were starting to move around and had coffee. We noticed she wasn't moving. Eboni tried waking her, but she was not responding. My baby was gone. The words filled my mind, *do not to lose your peace and joy.* I knew then what God was telling me. He was saying a storm is coming, and it was going to be rough, but I must be strong for her children. That's how I took it. All my life, my job was to be strong, but this was different. I was in shock for many days, just going through the motions. Phaedra and the family were trying to comfort me, and I was trying to comfort her children.

Phaedra and Bridgitte were very close. Bridgitte was the big sister who was there for her as a child and while growing up. It was devastating for her. We all looked to Bridgitte for different things. She was our rock in so many ways. It was a sad day. I gathered strength from God. He comforted me through it all. The Holy Spirit was always allowing me to feel His presence. He said, "I will never leave you or forsake you." I know why now He made sure I understood then as to what He was saying even when I didn't get it during that time. He knew I would have His words to cling to and give me the strength to hold on to, and not lose my mind. He loves me so much to let me know what was happening, but you must be secure and fixed on Him. The first couple of weeks after Bridgitte's death, I was hurting and grieving so bad, but with each passing day, I understood it better.

I woke up one morning trying to go to work after taking a few weeks off. I was off balance and my head ached so much. I had a headache already for many days, but that morning it was worse. I tried to move around, or sit on the toilet, then it hit me that my equilibrium was off, and vertigo had taken over. I was still trying to make it. Phaedra came in to check on me and by then, I just fell into her arms and told her I needed to go to the emergency room because something was wrong. After the CT scan and many exams, the doctors concluded that the shock of my daughter's death had elevated my stress level. The doctor came back into the room with two gigantic needles, and I asked, "What the heck is all that for?" She said one was for the vertigo, and the other was a very potent medication for the pain. Afterwards, I was released, and the doctor told Phaedra to take me home and put me to bed. I was out of it for hours, and when I finally came out of it, the headache and vertigo was gone. I was almost myself again so, the next day, I went back to work. I was trying to be okay but emotionally I wasn't. I'd either go to the bathroom or my car and weep.

I had gone to my car hurting so bad that God sent an angel to let me know I wasn't alone. It was Edie on my cell. Most often, she would call me on the work number. Her comforting words were angelic and soothing. They were just like my Pastor Linda's when she would call; her voice was always soft and supportive. It helped me tremendously that day. It was hard to go long periods of time without grieving. Another time I had to leave work because I was crying convulsively. I could feel that vertigo feeling coming back and the headaches were already present. I went to the bathroom and talked to God asking Him to please help me during my hurting time. While speaking with God, it was almost like I could hear my daughter say, "Mom, please stop hurting yourself, you must be strong for yourself, and the family, and that she didn't want my health to get worse." I couldn't visually see her, but hearing her voice was real to me. I didn't understand how I was speaking to God, and then my daughter was there. Some would probably say that it was Bridgitte there talking to me, but I know it was God and not my daughter.

Many years later in Grief-Share, a grief recovery support group designed by my church, Living Praise Christian Center, for those that were in need of help and healing over losing a loved one. In one of the meetings, Pastor Ayers, one of our grief counselors, made it so clear for me. We were discussing familiar spirits. Some in the group thought their loved ones could come back, but many of us knew they couldn't because the Bible says the gulf is too wide. (Luke 16:26, KJV) Pastor Ayers said, "God is so loving that when He sees us hurting, He will do whatever it takes to help us during that time." He said all things are possible with God if we just believe." Pastor Ayers' words put it all together for me.

God is a great God. He knew just what I needed to hear. I was a new person. I knew if I continued down the road I was on, it would lead to dangerous health issues. From that point on, I was able to be in control of my grieving. When I get too far out there, I think of the pleasant memories we had. My mind goes back to the good times we had in raising our children, some good, some not. It all goes together.

As you have read, when I'm done, I'm finished. I am laughing and thanking God. I know I will always hurt, but I know how to turn that hurt around. I rethink it before it gets me down where I can't come back sane and healthy. I had seen this happen with two of my friends after they lost their children. I focus on John 14:27, "Peace I leave with you, my peace I give unto you. Let not your heart be troubled, neither let it be afraid." God gave me peace in my darkest hour. The peace and joy that He said not to lose, If He said it, I must try very hard to keep it.

Chapter Seventeen

MY CHURCH

I must take a time to talk about my church during the worse time of my life. When my season was over at Faithful Central Church in Inglewood, I had to find a church in the valley. Phaedra and I were members of Faithful Central Church for many years. She was in the choir and head of the drama ministry. I was in the counseling department working with the ministry "Healing for Damaged Emotions" for women. We were on the 405 freeway three to four times a week. It was terrific for many years and before I had a retinal detachment. I had to decide to find a church home in the valley. It was hard leaving Faithful Central and my good friends.

After my eye surgery, I knew I had to leave Faithful Central and I was okay with it. While visiting many churches, someone told me about Living Praise Christian Center (LPCC). I decided to check it out. A few of the churches I had visited tried hard to get me to join after hearing my testimony of riding through the storm with Jesus. I enjoyed the churches but wasn't feeling it enough to make it my church home. After being at Faithful Central and under Bishop Ulmer, I knew it would be hard to find another pastor who was honest and could bring the word straight from the Bible. When I walked in the door God said, "This is where you pay your tithes." That meant to me that it was my church home. The first time I met the pastors, I shared with them that I'd been serving at

Faithful Center, under the leadership of Bishop Kenneth Ulmer for many years. I said to them that I felt Bishop Ulmer was a realist and an anointed man of God and it would take a mighty man to match up to him. Yes, I did say that. Pastor Hodge told me that he would do his best.

After a few more Sunday services and Wednesday night Bible studies, I went and told him he had lived up to his word and I thanked God for leading me to LPCC, and the opportunity to be taught by a pastor who loves the Lord. He is a man of God who teaches the word from the Bible and truly loves his sheep. He shows it in all his teachings. I knew it was what I needed. Before closing his message, Pastor Hodge would say, "Give me a year and see how you feel." It doesn't take a year to see the dedication, commitment, and the anointing that he has on his life, and all ministry leaders under him have that same commitment. They are the best teachers and pastors I have ever seen. Their teaching is phenomenal. Pastor Linda has a heart for hurting women. The pastors are transparent about their raw and real-life experiences. God allowed them to go down some devastating roads with many turns, some good, and some not so good but, it was preparation for their ministry today.

When Bridgitte went home to be with the Lord, they called Phaedra and me to their office and asked, "what can we do for you?" I was overwhelmed, I never had pastors be there for me, and my family. They assisted us in many areas, and our church members took care of the repast. They turned my recreation room into a beautiful place for our guests, thanks to Lady Antoinette Bell. There were phone calls for several days coming from Pastor Linda which were angelic, very soothing, and comforting. I am so grateful for my church, and I love my pastors and church family so much. I appreciate them as well and will be forever grateful for God placing me in their care. Pastor always says he loves us, and thankful to God for putting us in his care. He knows he will have to answer to God, so his teaching is insightful, current, and revelatory. Pastor Hodge is a remarkable man of God. He passed the test.

Phaedra and I had gone through many strange and hurting times with each passing family members. It was time to get away again. There was another cruise that LPCC had put together. This time we would be on the world's largest cruise ship on the high seas. The cruise featured water shows, theme parks, cantinas, casino, several restaurants, ice skating, zip lining, nightclubs, fabulous theaters, and many shopping stores. The ship had fourteen floors, one of which was designed just like New York Central Park with real grass, and birds chirping. The Lido deck on the top was always open fun, every hour something was going on. It was unbelievable and incredible. The Lord blessed us with this unimaginable cruise that gave us time to reflect, relax, have fun, and see some of the beauty that He created.

On our first day, cruising to the Bahamas, a young lady went overboard. One gentleman said he was praying and looked up, and saw the young lady falling. Our trip started off with sadness, and we didn't know how or what happened, we just knew a mother lost her child. I could relate. The captain turned the ship around and headed back. And the coast guards had the ocean lit up. I think everyone knew it was too late to do anything. It was unfortunate, but she was gone when she hit the water. I knew the captain went against orders turning that ship around, but he had compassion for the parents and did it anyway. It was a sad night for everyone, however, the next day was better as we got back in the vacation mood and started to have fun.

I had been to St. Thomas and many of the other Islands before, but never with Phaedra, so it was extra special being with her on the trip. We had a wonderful time together, and it was lovely to fellowship with some of our church family. We had dinner every night with our pastors and friends, and we were able to see the other side of the dynamic couple who had embraced us during those dark days. It was such a blessing.

When we pulled into the Bahamas, everyone started shouting and screaming with excitement. None of us could imagine what was going on. Men in uniform were on the shore saluting our ship. I still didn't get it until I saw three other ships arriving. Our ship was the largest and overshadowed the others. Many of us had never seen one that size before. Like I said before, ours was the largest in the world. This trip was just what the doctor ordered. We knew God had given us much favor. It wasn't cheap but having a year to make payments allowed us to be a part of something so fascinating.

Chapter Eighteen

THE MIRACULOUS HEALING

Moving along and getting back to the so-called "norm." The job was getting better with much support from my friends. After we prayed, it became a more peaceful atmosphere, and that cruel supervisor was no longer there. We had freedom and less tension. A new person came into the department, named Rose, and we found out her daughter had passed right after graduating high school. God strategically placed all of us together. There were four of us in the department that had to say "goodbye" to our children including our director. God knew we would need each other to encourage, support, and gain strength from each other. One can never say, "I know what you are going through," unless they have been through the same thing. So, we all cried and gave thanks together. When one of us was having a rough time, we were there to love on that person, pray, or be with them. God had already setup and prepared us for a time such as that.

I'd been feeling sick from the Hepatitis C virus and sometimes it would get me down for days, but it wasn't too much out of the norm, because I was sickly since childhood. The doctors thought I had polio because of the symptoms of weakness in my legs, fever, chills, and fatigue all at one time. I was in the hospital for weeks, and they ran many tests, but nothing was found. As a child, I always enjoyed the trips to the hospital because I would get milk and delicious food three times a day along with snacks at night. It just seemed my body was off at times.

The symptoms I was having at this time were much like those I had way back when I was drinking and having hangovers. I would get sick, and I would always ask God to please let me be well enough to be in my post as a greeter at church. I took my ministry job very seriously. Most of the time God made sure I was okay. Many other times, I would be sick up to Saturday night. I would be praying to be okay for Sunday morning. Most often, when I opened my eyes, I would feel the sickness had passed or was passing on. God has never left me. His presence has been real in my life. He heard me every time I cried and prayed.

My doctors always had some treatment they wanted me to try for the virus, and by the time they finish explaining it, I would reject the treatment. I would tell them God has a better plan for me and He does not want me to take weekly injections for a year and be sick for days from the treatment. These episodes were like being on a roller coaster ride and by the time I would be feeling better, it would be time for another shot. Not for me, no thanks. So, in December 2015, my doctor called me in to tell me they had a new treatment. It was a breakthrough treatment that was taking the medical world by storm called Harvoni®. One pill a day for three months with very few side effects. They also told me, had I tried the other treatment, I wouldn't have qualified for Harvoni®. *Look at my God.* The positive side effect of Harvoni® was after fourteen days the virus is gone. However, for extra protection, my doctors wanted me to take it for three months. It is a miracle drug, and God was in charge. Make no mistakes about it, the cost is approximately one hundred dollars a pill, and so many were not able to get the treatment.

I said yes right away, thinking of (Jeremiah 29:11). "For I know the plans, I have for you. One not to harm you, but to prosper you, and give you hope for a future." It's one of my favorite scripture in the Bible. I always knew that God would heal me of the virus. I had faith in Him. I agreed and followed the treatment. I didn't have to think about it this time. It was as if God said, "This is it." As my doctor and nurse continued to lay out the plan, they opened a file drawer with hundreds of patient's files indicating those patients were far worse with the virus than I was but couldn't afford the treatment. Praise God, with my insurance and the senior advantage coverage, I could. I thanked the Lord for His favor, grace, and mercy. He favored me for that matter. I started the treatment on the eleventh of December 2015. My fourteenth day was on Christmas. It was the most beautiful present our Lord and Savior gave to me. I have faith in God, and I knew He had a plan for me. Jeremiah had reminded me of that, for many years.

Christmas day was over the top with the healing I had going on inside of me. It was an out of body experience, very spiritual and transforming. God was doing great things for me, and that connection was so peaceful. My soul and mind were on a spiritual high. The gift of healing I received was so precious, and my God wanted me to know He was right there with me every step of the way. He said, "I rejoice with you, and I would never leave you or forsake you. You believed in me. You had faith that, I would heal you. You stood on your faith and trust, and for that you are healed." It was just that deep. The Lord touched me on that Christmas day, which I will remember forever.

On the ninth of January, I went for my follow-up, and my doctor was so excited about the results. She asked me had I seen them online to which I told her, "No." The doctor was shocked and asked, "Why not?" I shared with her that I knew I was healed and didn't need to check. She looked at me sideways as I professed a strong faith in the Lord. What I had been telling them all along came to pass. She pulled it up, and it read, "NO VIRUS FOUND." It was a moment of pure joy for both of us. I had a chance to witness the goodness and faithfulness of the Lord. The total treatment was ninety-five thousand dollars and I didn't pay a penny. My doctor said to me that I was one lucky lady. I said to her, "luck didn't have anything to do with it. I was a blessed woman of God and the King's kid."

Chapter Nineteen

THE LITTLE BROWN ONE

This book is about my life and my testimony of the many ways God has blessed and kept His word. He was with me every step, every journey, and new adventure throughout my life. There were many angels along the way. I wouldn't have made it if angels weren't dispatched along the way for me. Many times, I heard Him speaking and sometimes not. It still blows my mind that when I didn't hear Him, He didn't hold it against me. He still loved me.

Being forced to go to church as a young person affected the way I viewed the church as a young person. I didn't go to church after leaving "the Giant" for a long time. Seeing the preacher that married Joe and me, left a bad taste in my mouth. That mistake caused me to have regrets about not raising my children in church. God planted the seed in me at an early age at the church when He spoke, telling me I knew of Him and loved Him, but with the toxic thinking and ugly environment around me, it didn't allow me to have the relationship I have with Him today. I had to grow into it. That's when I was able to see the blessings unfolding, feeling His presence, and being guided by His love. The name of the Lord is a strong tower: the righteous runs in it and is safe (Proverb 18:10). I didn't understand a lot of it until I was older and broken. After seeking a relationship with our Lord and Savior, He then began to reveal His presence.

While writing this book, there were many times I would get discouraged, and wanted to stop writing. One day God told me, "It's not just about you, but of the many times, I have blessed you. Your many testimonies could be a blessing to many." So, I would continue to write. There were many sad times, many happy, and many angry and cuts to the heart moments. I cried so many times remembering all of this stuff. It was cleansing in many areas, and I gained insight on so much. Had I not written my story, I never would have realized who my real daddy was. God showed all that to me, and for that, I am truly grateful. I have repented for so many things that I did and asked for forgiveness for the things that I didn't do well.

There was still so much more to write, but some things are best to stay buried. When God says it's time, I will share more, but you got the best of me, well, most of it. I didn't share about my mean streak. That apple can't fall too far from the tree and not have some of its mother's flavor. Most of the time, I have been pleasant, but I could cut you with words or looks. I was well aware of my mean, hurtful streak. I never had time for foolishness. I probably never handled that well. Phaedra told me one day, several times that I was mean and didn't manage situations well. As she was saying this to me, I'm thinking, "the same of you." Phaedra is so much like me and holds onto things that happened in the past. I believe she forgives but has a hard time forgetting. She and I have had some hard battles. For many years we loved as hard as we fought. She wants me to be a certain way, and as I try to explain to her, I am who I am. I will try to be the best that I can be, but I can't undo those times that bad things happened.

Phaedra hates drinking and drugs, the two things that caused so much pain in our family. I missed her eight-grade graduation. I was in Detroit and had hung out too much the night before and missed my plane. I don't think she ever got over that. I am sure this is just one of many times that play in her head when we are at it. These are things we must let go. She once said to me, that it took years for me to forgive my mother and I should let her have her time. I don't want her to hurt or suffer as I did. I want her to stand on the scripture, "Therefore, if any man be in Christ, he is a new creature: old things are passed away; behold, all things become new." (2 Corinthians 5:17) I would like her to see me as that new creature and know all that old stuff have passed away. Those old days are gone, and it's a new day. Let us rejoice and be glad in it.

It took years for me to see my ways. I had to always keep my guard up while raising my little village. I believed, if you were weak, people would walk over you. I am softer now but will make a statement if I must.

One thing I learned about myself was the way I held on to stuff that should have been released immediately. I was talking to one of my first best friends, Gladys, in Detroit and I was sharing something with her in a laughing manner. I was telling her about one of my friends, who is closer than a sister. Yet and still, we bumped heads, all thirty years of our friendship. It was ugly in the early part of our friendship, and God just kept bringing us back together, like the seashell that keeps washing up on the shore. He was reminding us, like the Bible says, "He who began a good work will be faithful to complete it." God let us know, it wasn't about us. He had a bigger plan for each of us, to be a blessing and not harm. He wanted us to be there to encourage each other, not put each other down. It took time to see God's plan for our life. She would get on my nerves, and I would get on hers. As we grew closer together in the Lord, she was able to release quicker than me.

I was telling Gladys how I would hold onto it much longer. Out of the blue, Gladys said, "You used to do me that way, get mad and not speak to me for days." That blew my mind. She was telling me I did that fifty years ago, and I was still doing it from time to time. My pastor was teaching on transformation, and he was parked on my street. I knew at that moment that I had to transform my thinking altogether. It was the greatest awakening for me. Clearing the wreckage of my path has helped me to be a better person and for that I am grateful.

After my conversation with Gladys, my mind wandered back to the day she told me that Jerome had died in Chicago in a basement all alone. I also thought about the last time I spoke with him. I was coming from Detroit, and he was trying to get me to layover in Chicago and be with him for a night. I refused all his pleading. I came home thinking, when I am finished, I am done. I didn't think much about it even when she told me he had passed.

Months later, I was coming from San Diego with Phaedra driving, and Tia in the front seat. I was stretched out on the back seat. We were rolling, having fun listening to Phaedra's collection of beautiful love songs. Suddenly, I started crying. I had a blanket over my head because the windows were down. I cried for my friend all the way from San Diego to the San Fernando Valley. My heart was hurting so badly, and I was hurting for my friend, but also for the person, I had become. I had not taken time to cry for this man. Yes, he had pissed me off by the lifestyle he led all the years we were together. But the fact was that we had been friends and lovers all those years. He treated me like the square girl that didn't have to give him money and support him. I knew his lifestyle and agreed to accept it. He was there helping me financially when my mama died, and for that, I owed him more than I gave him. He always dressed me in the best, the top of the line raw silk suits, Persian lamb coats. I was sharp. Plus, Jerome was a help to me in so many other ways like purchasing my homes and taking care of my children.

The fact that I had grown so cold, and that I didn't cry for my friend, made me see just how ugly I could be. I repented and asked God to please forgive me. I didn't know if he was saved and that was hurtful. For years after that I prayed that he was okay and in heaven. I think I owed him that much to say a few words about my friend. Jerome Adams, my friend and my lover for many years. May you rest in peace. Tears can be more special than smiles because smiles can be given to anyone, but tears are only shed for the ones we love.

As my friend, my daughter, Bridgitte would say, "a friend knows all your best stories. A good friend has lived them with you." I know God has a purpose for my pain, a reason for my struggle, and a gift for my faithfulness. I also am confident that choices and consequences come in a package deal. When we make a choice, we ignite the consequences that come along with it. I have made many bad choices and had to pray myself out of them. I have gained strength by overcoming obstacles. I possess the power to overcome adversities. God made sure of that.

For that, I dedicate my life to Him. With His help, I was able to unmask many areas that I wouldn't have dared to uncover. I was birthed by a mama who didn't want children. She enjoyed being in the company of men but didn't have a form of birth control. I felt rejection at a very early age as it left me with feelings of not being wanted, nor loved.

My past and present circumstances do not dictate my future anymore. Knowing now, without the trials and tribulations, I wouldn't have the gift of testimonies. I am in abundance now, planting new seeds and bearing new fruit. I am starting a whole new life. New things are on my plate. So many new places to visit. I will always be in His presence.

Still Standing, The Little Brown One!

About the Author

At the age of fifteen, Willie Frances Hill was forced to marry her husband who was nine years her senior. During the three-year marriage, she gave birth to a son and a daughter. Willie devoted her life to taking care of and supporting her sisters, her three children, grandchildren, nieces, nephews, and many more. She often thought and said, "Who else is going to do it?" Willie worked many jobs to accomplish her mission. She had a long career in the Aerospace industry while also working as a counselor to abused women, and an alcohol and chemical abuse counselor. Retired, she is an active member of her church, Living Praise Christian Center in Chatsworth, California and she resides in Southern California.

Made in the USA
San Bernardino, CA
20 June 2019